SNIPPETS OF
A LIFE MOSTLY LIVED

True Stories in 85 Syllables

A Haiku Memoir

Dan Dana

© Dan Dana, 2022

Five Palms Press
Sarasota, Florida
dandana.us/fivepalms

DEDICATION

My Relief Generation

nearing the hand-off
of my lap with the baton
your turn has begun

our story's passed on
distant past to far future
one life at a time

shrouded in folklore
memory's fleeting half-life
decays to nothing

save this slim box of
Papi's memory snippets
for your relievers

as future unfurls
preserve your lap's key moments
the relay goes on

With Seamus and Claribel in 2006

PREFACE

I Forgot to Ask

Grandpa, where were you
when the First World War broke out?
I forgot to ask

Grandma, tell me tales
about my great-grandmother.
I forgot to ask

Dad, how did you choose
your career, and your first wife?
I forgot to ask

Mom, what did you like
about Dad when you first met?
I forgot to ask

kids, I'm getting old
anything you'd like to know?
don't forget to ask

My mom on her final birthday, 2008

PREAMBLE

My Schizoid Compromise*

how close do I come,
daring to let you see me
—*real* me, warts and all?

and, how far away
do I keep hidden from you,
safe from your arrows?

writing this memoir,
now shared on the world wide web,
reveals my answer

browsing these snippets,
you may peer into my self
through frosted windows

I'm only human,
managing my boundaries,
just like you, my friend

---

* A term from object relations theory, developed by psychoanalyst Melanie Klein

Grandmother Dana with my dad (top center) and siblings, circa 1900

Gant grandparents with my mom and two of her five brothers, circa 1919

§

I'm getting old. Although in good health and seeing no lethal storm clouds on the near horizon, the finitude of my life has been made starkly evident by the quickening pace of the years speeding by.

This memoir contains haiku quintets that depict events in my life from earliest memories to the present. As such, they represent a body of family history for many. My daughter is my only child. Having two rather prolific siblings, I am known as "Uncle Dan" by some seventy people. Having even more fruitful grandparents, I am "Cousin Dan" to hundreds spread throughout the United States. Go back a few more generations, and my family tree includes many thousands more distant cousins, perhaps sharing a branch with you. Some of my life-snippets may intersect with your own memories or remind you of stories you've heard 'round the family table.

Even more broadly, my immigrant roots date from the landing of the *Mayflower* in 1620 and are shared by tens of thousands of distant American cousins. So, *my* family history may also be *your* family history. (Curiously, my wife Susan and I recently discovered a common ancestor born in 1670, making us eighth cousins.)

What's a haiku quintet, you ask? Rooted in ancient Japanese poetry, this adapted form consists of five stanzas of three lines, each having five, seven, and five syllables, respectively, summing to 85 syllables. A photo or image illustrates and completes the finished piece. This derivative structure is my own humble creation. The "life snippet" variant reports actual events as I recall them.

Many evenings at sunset and in its afterglow, when not preempted by some pesky obligation, I sit at our west window watching the daily "sunset movie" (a different show each night), headphones in place, listening to music chosen to complement my mood, a glass of decent cabernet near at hand. The plot is predictable, but the cinematography is gorgeous.

Immersed in this multi-sensory beauty, memory-snippets sometimes bob to the surface of my mind, posing for inspection. Aware that life's clock is ticking toward midnight, I snag these ephemeral critters before they slip back into memory's murky depths. I wordsmith each one into the shape of a haiku quintet and put it in a box for safekeeping.

This memoir is that box.

Relatives might enjoy riffling through the box for curious bits of our shared family story. Non-relatives might stumble upon triggers of your own life-snippets.

Browse. Let your mind wander. Follow it there. Repeat.

CONTENTS

Part 1—Life Snippets—tells true stories in chronological order as they occurred—*Page 1*

Part 2—Susan—celebrates my wife. As the muse and frequent subject of my poetic reveries, life-partner Susan deserves a special place in this collection. These poems are not about events per se that can be listed chronologically, but nonetheless represent a central feature of my experience. As my steady companion since 1995, she was present and involved in most of the snippets reported in Part 1 since our pairing. Together, we have crafted a model relationship that may serve as a helpful touchstone for others. Certain ingredients of our secret sauce are revealed—*Page 103*

Part 3—Roots—digs deeper. Several immigrant ancestors who first ventured from Europe to North America established familial lines that lead directly to me. One Native American links my DNA to the first human inhabitants of the Western Hemisphere over 15,000 years ago. Haiku about Viking and African roots probe pre-history—*Page 127*

Part 4—Death—contemplates the end. To write one's memoir suggests that the writer's life has been mostly lived. I am 77 years old and cannot dispute that conclusion. Meanwhile, I remain in the arena and continue playing the game—*Page 137*

Part 5—The Future—reflects upon today's inflection point in American history with a worried eye toward the world that my grandchildren, and their grandchildren, may inherit—*Page 155*

Part 6—Write Your Own—is for readers who sense their own looming mortality and wish to leave a record for posterity. Some kind of snippet—perhaps the haiku quintet form—is suggested as a more expedient option than traditional narrative storytelling—*Page 159*

About me—*Page 163*

1
LIFE SNIPPETS

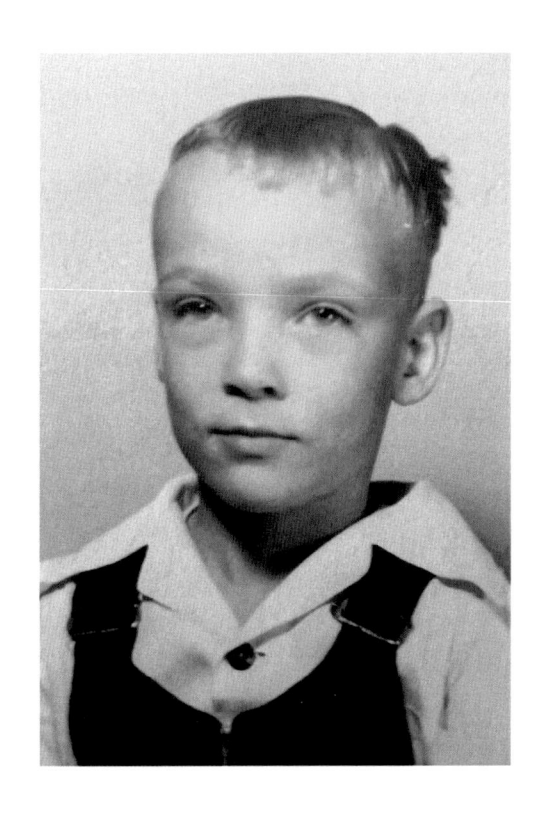

MY BIRTH

I was a preemie
not ready for life outside,
or so I was told

siblings were stronger
my frail five pounds weighed on Mom
she'd practiced on them

somehow, I made it
earned farm-boy immunities
fending nature's bugs

long before the Pill
I was my dad's eighth and last
spanning five decades

thanks, Mom and Daddy
for giving me life to live
I might have not been

November 1945

Great-grandmother's diary entry 23 September 1945: "Dan born at 1 am"

MY MOM

25 December 1918 – 15 September 2009

Christmas-born baby
sturdy hardscrabble farm-folk
third of six, five boys

learned love from Grandma
sacrificed past my knowing
selflessness unseen

music, prized heirloom
kindness, greatest gift of all
I sip from her depth

I claim no esteem
by genes and her example
she created me

village raises child
nature's treasures I'm bequeathed
but first, my mother

Bradford Louise Gant Dana, circa 1919

MY DAD

14 December 1874 - 22 April 1955

on this Father's Day
you're one-hundred-forty-six
your last child salutes

totem of my youth
aspirational model
pedestal figure

dwindling few of us
remember your twinkling eyes
what thoughts stirred your mind?

when I reach your years
who'll recall my twinkling eyes?
some aging poet?

meanwhile, life goes on
I'm busy living each day
just as you were, Dad

J. W. Dana, circa 1919

THE GRASSHOPPER PLAGUE

when I was a boy
my dad told me this story
he was an old man:

"they filled the whole sky
they turned the daylight to dark
they sounded like rain

they smothered our farm
they stripped the leaves from corn stalks
they ate our garden

we burned them in piles
we smashed them, but not enough
they left us hungry"

I cherish his tale
passing it along to you
I'm the old man now

Near Humboldt, Kansas, 1874, his birthplace and birthyear
Image source: Kansas Historical Society

MY DAD AND ROOSEVELT

story he told us
now faded like clippings from
the local paper:

*on a rainy day
at John Brown's memorial
I met Roosevelt*

*as a party man
I welcomed the President
to my Kansas town*

hanging by a shred
this bit of family lore
would have turned to dust

but it's now preserved
for one more generation
in today's haiku

Theodore Roosevelt arriving in Osawatomie, Kansas, to deliver a speech on 31 August 1910 at a memorial for abolitionist John Brown. J.W. Dana was a local Republican Party official at that time.
   Photo source: Kansas Historical Society

WHY MY NAME IS DAN

I am third of three
Deana and Jon came first
then I joined the clan

what to name this one?
Dad proposed "Cornelius,"
—his own spurned birth name!

"no child of mine—no!"
Mom put her foot down squarely
I thank her muchly

his next idea:
"I had little brother Dan,
Jon should have one, too"

that's what I was told
by my Mom, who surely knew
why my name is Dan

Uncle Dan Dana (1881-1964)

KNOXVILLE

wide place in the road
no stop sign to slow traffic
two miles east of home

Cox General Store
old men spit chew on the porch
hitching post nearby

Charley's blacksmith shop
forged horse shoes and gate hinges
pounding his anvil

Yoakum's gas station
Sindy's greasy repair shop
church, one-room schoolhouse

my rear-view mirror
reflects these seventy years
down Highway Thirteen

Knoxville, Missouri, population ~ 30 in the 1950's
Photo: Revisiting Knoxville, March 15, 2022

MAPLE TREE

I found your young sprout
across Skunk Creek, up the lane
amid roadside brush

sister De helped me
transplant you to our back yard
near the cherry tree

how tall will you grow?
will you be here when I die?
how will my life end?

the boy sought answers
to impossible questions,
setting his life's path

I left home, you're stuck
we've grown these seven decades
will we meet again?

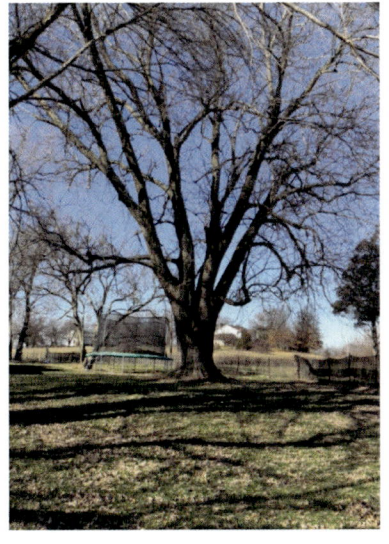

My childhood home near Knoxville, circa 1951
Photo: Maple tree at age 70, 6 December 2021

WRAPPED IN STRING

at our stone fireplace
my dad read his newspaper
warming his old bones

he sat in silence
pretending not to notice
I wrapped him in string

"time for bed, you boys"
I thought I had him tied down
up the stairs we went

first thing next morning
I could hardly wait to see
if he was still there

string was on the floor
Dad's at the breakfast table
how did he get loose?

Mom, Dad, Jon, me (sister Deana took photo, circa 1953)

MILKING OLD RED

I milked her each night
head nestled in her warm flank
savoring her smell

Old Red chewed her cud
surely glad to be relieved
her swollen bag eased

squeezing teats top-down
Tom meowing for a fresh squirt
then I took a turn

drafty barn door slats
slowed Missouri's winter wind
cow's warmth dulled its bite

my daily chore done
lugged sloshing bucket homeward
wider world called me

Family farm near Knoxville, 1951-1955
Photo source: wisconsinhistory.org

GRANDMOTHER'S HOUSE

Sundays after church
dinner at Grandmother's house
fond weekly routine

Granddad was born there
sagging creaky floors, throw rugs
loved his strong cigars

chicken, spuds, green beans
hymns sung 'round the piano
four-part harmony

cousins, uncles, aunts
card games, pitch-and-catch
grown-ups talked, kids played

everyone's gone now
house burned down long ago
sometimes, I'm still there

Knoxville, 1945-1963. Photo circa 1957.
My 6th grade picture is taped to their wall (top left corner)

MINTING MONEY

I melted wheel weights
in cupped tongs at the fireplace
meant for stoking coals

pouring molten lead
on the hearth to make play coins
my wealth grew nightly

inscribing each one
by hammer and screwdriver
to show year minted

rounding their edges
to perfect my creations
for posterity

those priceless lead coins
did not survive growing up
would be worth gold now

The fireplace hearth in my childhood home near Knoxville, 1950's
Image source: Unknown (similar but not original)

EDDA

my primal playmate
cotton dolls 'neath grandmas' quilts
church-basement Wednesdays

no nearby age-peers
country schoolmarm taught us well
square dance romance throbbed

our mothers had plans?
timid shyness kept me mum
but fantasies roared

Mizzou brought new worlds
each found our own path onward
fleeting decades passed

Sarasota lunch
glad to see you, oldest friend!
you've not changed, have I?

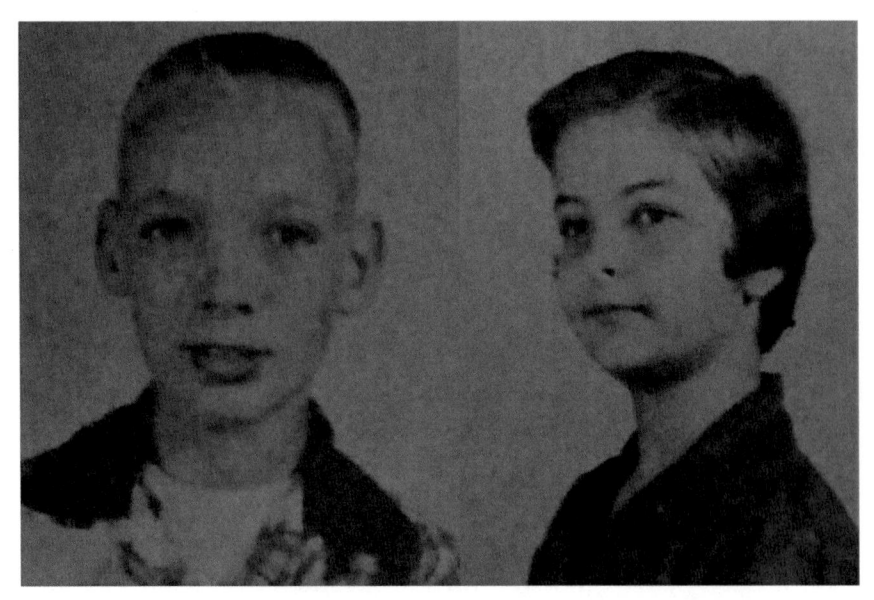

Class photos: Knoxville two-room school, 1956
Reunion at Columbia restaurant, Sarasota, 2018

UNDERESTIMATING MY MOM

I fancied myself
a fast runner, at age nine
could I beat my mom?

she took my challenge
to the far mulberry tree
she easily won

I was deflated
she hugged me with love and grace
I learned a lesson

in whatever field
underestimate my mom
at your own peril

for years thereafter
she was sorry for winning
love's the real lesson

Setting my childhood home, circa 1954
Photo: Displaying another of her remarkable talents at age 89, April 2008

MY DAD'S EARTHLY AFTERLIFE

smoking was not blamed
no one knew it was cancer
that was killing him

coughing up dark blood
he got sick in mid-winter
did he see ahead?

I am his youngest
us kids stayed with Grandmother
to shield us, I s'pose

last time I saw him
snaked tubes in oxygen tent
he was not moving

and then he was gone …
glimpsed in wistful, wishful dreams
he still breathes in me

Photo: J. W. Dana (12/14/1874 – 4/22/1955) with family, 11 June 1952

ODE TO MRS. MASON

seventh grade teacher
taught all subjects with finesse
classroom held four grades

farmland country school
sentence diagramming fun
weekly spelling bee

just carrots, no sticks
blackboard performances cheered
errors gently coached

seedbed sown with care
career trajectory launched
my sprout has grown tall

sixty-five years hence
living still, in this haiku
thank you, Mrs. Mason

Photo: Knoxville school 1956-57
Mrs Mason: bottom row, second from left; Me: top row, center

PRICE AND ME

we were a good team
mowing pastures, plowing corn
manning our John Deere's

laughing and waving
back and forth across the field
every time we passed

I was young, he's old
he seemed happy as our hand
I never thought twice

Price "knew his place" there
always friendly, always kind
in our Jim Crow land

never shared a meal
he never entered our home
Price was Black, you see

In fond memory of Price Cunningham
Ray County Missouri, 1953-1963 (photo source unknown)

I TRIED

I read the bible
I listened to Pastor Bob
I pushed down my doubts

each Sunday morning
I sat still, as expected
waiting for the light

Jews are confident
Catholics are sure they're right
Muslims too, I'm told

Mom said to have faith
I feared the torture of Hell
"could I deserve that?"

my weak faith faltered
I tried to make sense of it
in the end, I failed

Setting: Knoxville Methodist Church, 1945-1960
Photo: The abandoned church of my childhood, March 15, 2022

BERTRAND RUSSELL
(1872-1970)

your words set me free
scales fell from wide teen-age eyes
young life's course re-set

superstitions foiled
country church's grip released
dogma's chains broken

freethought flowed freely
in secular humanism's
sensible worldview

these sixty years hence
I ponder the Universe
in your wise shadow

your book filled its task
enriched life beyond measure
thank you, Lord Russell

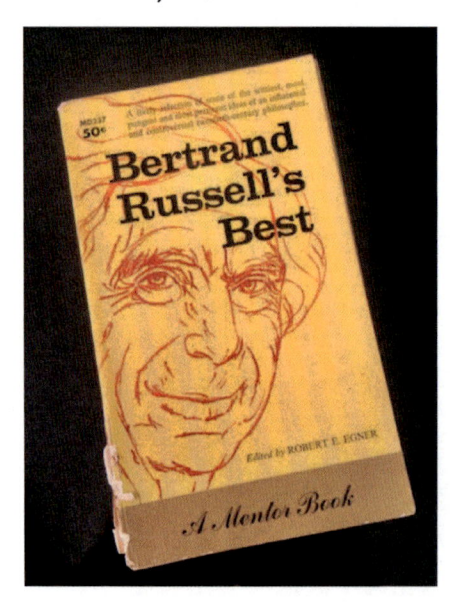

Photo: Original personal copy of the book that changed my life in 1961

THE CHICKEN

on the dusty road
by old neighbor Henry's farm
a slow chicken died

three silage truckers
sped by many times that day
smashing that chicken

each time a welcome
moment of fun distraction
on a boring day

by evening only
feathers and brown smudge remained
to mark its flat grave

chuckling at day's end
we three shared chicken stories
in fowl disrespect

Setting: The gravel road between cornfield and pit silo on our family farm, Ray County, Missouri, August 1962
Image source: shutterstock

MOWING ALFALFA

that pivotal day
summer before senior year
to farm was the plan

mowing alfalfa
was my chore, and my future
by noon, life transformed

lightning struck that day
a jolt of empowerment
"I can change the plan!"

dropping FFA
enrolling at Ole Mizzou
my new field was math

fickle plans took me
through six rewarding decades
to greener pastures

Ray County, Missouri, family farm, summer 1962
Photo source: youtube (similar tractor and mower)

JFK IS DEAD

playing hearts at noon
four guys on a dorm room bed
before chemistry

someone yelled out loud:
"the president has been shot!"
"of what?" I wondered

some students brought their
own transistor radios
to class, turned down low

he tried to teach, but
waved, "turn up your radios"
Cronkite: "he is dead"

prof openly sobbed
only then this moment in
history sunk in

Freshman year, Donnelly Hall, University of Missouri, 22 November 1963
Photo source: history.com

A DECISION DEFERRED

failing socially
failing in academics
failing with women

my future seemed bleak
happiness felt beyond reach
I despaired of hope

a flash of insight
suddenly brightened my mood:
I could end my life!

I'd found a way out
I could escape this prison
I was free to choose

so … do it today?
there's no rush, I decided
and there still isn't

Setting: Freshman year at University of Missouri, 1963-64
Photo: On a return visit to campus with Susan, 2019

HITCHHIKING

I've thumbed countless miles
Mizzou to Knoxville and back
weekend laundry runs

California called
to see a nameless girlfriend
after freshman year

our grand loop out west
sophomore summer junket
with dorm roommate Wayne

Michigan's U P
weekend AWOL excursion
from Indy's Fort Ben

it was safe back then
before the world went crazy
when trust was in vogue

The highways of America, 1963-1966

TET 1968

was I even there?
memories succumbed to age
or, suppressed by fear?

three stuporous nights
minigun fireworks traced sky
choppers pounded air

silent tunnel maze
beneath my senseless slumber
Viet Cong cooked rice

mortars shook death's door
fickle fate skipped my bunker
by pure random chance

today I wonder
this surreal lifetime later
was I even there?

Setting: Cu Chi Vietnam, January 31, 1968
Photo: Inside Viet Cong tunnel beneath Cu Chi, May 1, 2015

CLERKS RAN THE ARMY

good old Uncle Sam
in his paternal kindness
thought of everything

gave us GI's weeks
of Rest & Relaxation
in exotic lands

chartered flight, hotel,
poor man's VIP treatment
once per year, they said

a mere records clerk
went to Taiwan, Philippines,
and Singapore too

I could do favors
a "lost" reprimand, perhaps
clerks ran the army

Photo: In Taiwan on R&R leave from Vietnam, 1968

MAN OF THE WORLD

I longed to be grown
to escape childhood's stigma
a man of the world

innocence was shame
my boyhood's war with myself
hidden scars remain

you're well on your way
beyond me at your same age
wise beyond your years

your confidence shines
sure of your adequacy
you are my heart's pride

I'll dwell within you
as you follow time's arrow
a man of the world

Papi at 22   Seamus at 22
  (1968)   (2022)

GETTING SHORT

we started counting
the day we got in-country
how many days left?

serving our country?
our job was to stay alive
get home in one piece

days of typing forms
nights of music and good weed
"coffee" break boosters

"hey, how short are you?"
we always knew the number
"<u>F</u>uck <u>T</u>he <u>A</u>rmy, Jack!"

the bird's lifting off
Cam Ranh Bay's behind me now
gone back to the World

Camp Granite, 527th PSC, Qui Nhon, October 1967-October 1968

VIETNAM AFTERTHOUGHTS

I came and I went
different people, it seems
a fork in my road

opportunities
some seized, even more wasted
but what might have been?

death seemed far away
I never saw body bags
in my bunkered mind

war can be good, eh?
only lessons learned, too late,
in history books

war can be just, eh?
saved us from Hitler's Nazis
Vietnam, not so

Qui Nhon, 1968

FINDING MYSELF

wanting to get back
to where I had never been
to find my people

for three restless years
trapped in army's stifling cage
the world changed—me, too

I found some hippies
peaceniks on a peaceful beach
they seemed much like me

skinny-dipping fun
hitchhikers shared campfire tales
tripping on acid

old shackles cast off
I had heard of these people
now I could be one

Puerto Ángel, Oaxaca, Mexico, January 1969
Photo: Puerto Ángel beach today, source: windows10spotlight

MOTORCYCLE MISHAP

I rolled to a stop
in grass beside the asphalt
hearing myself groan

opening my eyes
bike lies beside me, running
it slid, undamaged

disc brakes had heated
rusty from months in storage
I flung myself off

escape tumbling bike
I thought the safer option
novice rider's goof

two passing farmers
in their dusty pick-up truck
stopped to rescue me

Pan-American highway (then a narrow asphalt road), near Nacaome, Honduras, January 1969. Photo 2020 same road, source: trip-suggest

MOTORCYCLE MISHAP SEQUEL

two weeks with two priests
recovering from mishap
scrapes and broken wrist

a friend of a friend
returned to scene of the crash
to check on my bike

a roadside peasant
had kept it from thieves and knaves
tethered by a string

his toe to its wheel
not knowing its true owner
each night for a month

doing his duty
honor-bound to keep it safe
wish I could thank him

Photo: A hut similar to the home of my motorcycle's caretaker
Source: Architectural League

MY TICKET TO RIDE

if no GI Bill
you would not be reading this
I'd be somewhere else

my ticket to ride
no other path would lead through
life's maze of crossroads

no teaching career
no MTI, no haiku,
no books on my shelf

no Susan, no Su,
no Seamus, no Claribel,
no Sarasota

counterfactuals
would have mapped my route
glad I wound up here

Photo 2022. I depended on GI Bill educational benefits for veterans from 1969 until completion of my PhD in 1977.

WOODSTOCK (GETTING THERE)

it was billed to be
"three days of peace and music"
—no mention of mud

three guys from Mizzou
toked our way through thick gray smoke
in Jack's old Plymouth

"a free festival"
New York radio broke news
free-for-all stampede

we parked miles away
planned to come back for our stuff
but crowd swept us up

no need for tickets
only the shirts on our backs
we plunged in, head first

Columbia MO to Bethel NY, August 1969
Photo: 2020 with original Woodstock tickets, framed

WOODSTOCK (BEING THERE)

rain soaked the first night
no refuge for wet hippies
we huddled masses

Arlo, Jimi, Sly
our pot-stoned mind-trip's soundtrack
joints toked, passed along

a more prepared girl
shared her soggy sleeping bag
shelter from the storm

making our own path
stepping over strewn bodies
to johns and bushes

in peace-and-love meme
I found my generation
it is called "Woodstock"

Woodstock Festival, Bethel, New York, August 15-17, 1969
Photo source: Google Sites

WOODSTOCK SOUVENIR

Jack googled my name
we'd shared trek to Yasgur's farm
long memory lane

his aging Plymouth
our ride to historic heights
powered by good weed

trampled fence opened
three days of mud and music
strewn bodies, stoned minds

peace-and-love stickers
happy humanists, our tribe
culture tacking left

we stumbled upon
one of life's sparkling jewels
life's a trip, eh Jack?

Jack in our Woodstock days

I ONCE SHOT A BIRD

old army pal Ron
asked me to go bird hunting
(I hate sport-killing)

we walked through the woods
our four-ten shotguns loaded
scanning trees for birds

Ron spied a sparrow
"take a shot," he pointed
reluctant, I did

she fell to the ground
we hurried to see my kill
pellet in her eye

"awwww, poor little bird"
"you'll never make a hunter"
so true, Ron, so true

Setting: Near Jefferson City MO, 1969(?). I fact-checked this poem with Ron, who questions its accuracy. My photo of Ron (right) and buddies overlooking Miraflores Locks near Fort Clayton, Panama Canal Zone, 1967

ESCAPING A KILLER

German car-runner
needed driver and Spanish
Belize-San José

"we're going there too"
he was an evil bastard
shooting roadside pigs

we feared his handgun
"let's escape at next border,
armed guards will protect"

"I will kill you, Dan!"
a trucker kindly took us
on to Managua

we hid on side streets
until sure he had passed through
then on to safe Zone

With Mary at Honduras-Nicaragua border, January 1972
Photo: After arriving in Panama Canal Zone

HELADO

not knowing the word
he tried to order ice cream
I offered to help

*"I've come to visit
a foster child I've not met"
"my first time down here"*

*"I need a driver
who speaks Spanish for this trip"*
I offered to help

for a grad student
seeking summer adventure
this was tailor-made

three days as his guide
my first interpreter gig
best ice cream ever!

Bogotá to Chiquinquirá, Colombia, summer 1972
Photo 2022: Holding the unstrung tiple I purchased from its maker in Chiquinquirá

ENCOUNTER GROUPS

we were eight strangers
exploring inner mindscapes
for twenty rich hours

known just by first names
pasts and futures cast aside
we stayed here-and-now

feelings outranked thoughts
urged to unveil our real selves
not the roles we play

challenged to own up
to submerged needs, shames, and fears
found we're much alike

I was a shy boy
feigning maturity while
trying to grow up

NTL Institute (Bethel, Maine) and other venues from 1972. I experienced, as member and leader, many personal growth groups and their variants during graduate school and beyond.

MY ONE NIGHT IN JAIL

middle of the night
police tapped on our window
we were fast asleep

unaware of law
"public sleeping" was a crime
in Conch Republic

Lucy's with putas
my cellmates were drug dealers
not our normal friends

break from summer school
two psychology students
collecting field notes

a farcical fluke
that spawned this haiku sitcom:
My One Night in Jail

Preparing for our drive to Key West (the "scene of the crime"), July 1973. My station wagon was furnished with a mattress and privacy curtains, but was declared "public sleeping" by local authorities.

REMEMBERING LUCY

friends, lovers, mentors
never bored—just start talking
psych was petri dish

Jamaican journey
did not fret our danger
dodged bullets with wits

Key West summer jaunt
sailboat, midnight leftovers,
Duval Street pool shark

Freud's ardent student
analysis was your thing
migrant of the mind

you left waaaay too soon
never got to say goodbye
you haunt my id, still

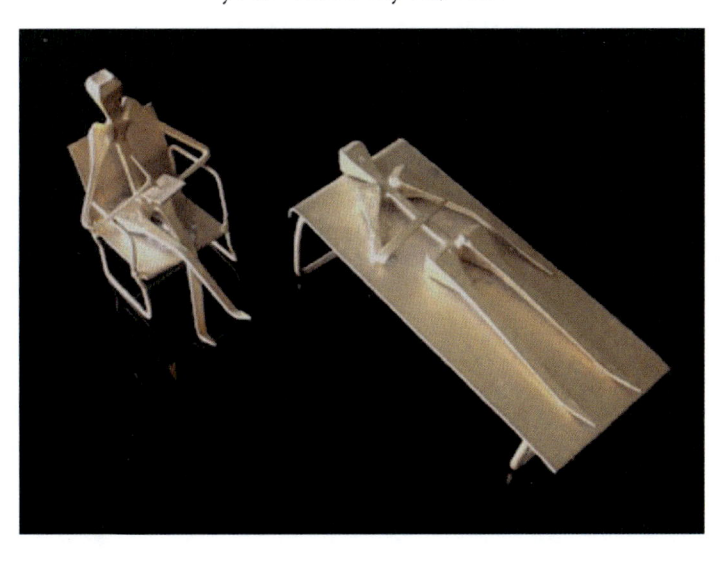

Lucy and I lived together 1974-1977 during graduate school and remained friends until she died in 2001. Photo: "The Witness" retrieved from Lucy's desk, now on mine.

DISCOVERING WORKPLACE MEDIATION

I'm new to this job:
resolving workplace conflict
as a third party

like couples, perhaps?
let them talk it out, don't quit
no advice-giving

they have sovereign choice
listen for peaceful gestures
"say more about that"

my job's not to fix
this magic process does it
I simply convene

mediation works
(without special credentials)
if I just let it

US Department of Education, Washington DC, late 1977, where I first adapted systems-theory couples counseling to workplace relationships, from which MTI's Manager-as-Mediator and related curricula evolved.

TEACHING LESSONS

"seven years and out"
I ignored tenure's dictum
self-employment called

teaching was my bridge
to goal of independence
my farm roots ran deep

soon found my focus:
how conflict plays with our minds,
how to win the peace

taught my final class
cut cord to holy paycheck
dangled by a thread

failure stalked my pride
life became my stern teacher
serving humble pie

Early teaching years, University of Hartford, 1978-1985

AMERICAN RUBLES

a fun course to teach
learning laboratory
a simulation

it felt real—and was
company of grad students
played corporate roles

performing real work
earning real compensation
to purchase their grade

produced case studies
about workplace behavior
for analysis

they did not get rich
in American Rubles
but they learned a lot

The "American Ruble" picturing Seamus was used as currency in the General Case Study Company classroom simulation, University of Hartford, 1979-2003 (artwork by Sean Connor)

MARATHON

not really a "race"
I had not trained hard enough
and I lacked talent

four slow hours and change
hit the wall at mile twenty
just as predicted

Woodstock 5-K "race"
one last dash for the daisies
finished next-to-last

"I might try again"
never got a round tuit
goals without plans fail

sour grapes suit my taste:
winning is overrated
life is not a race

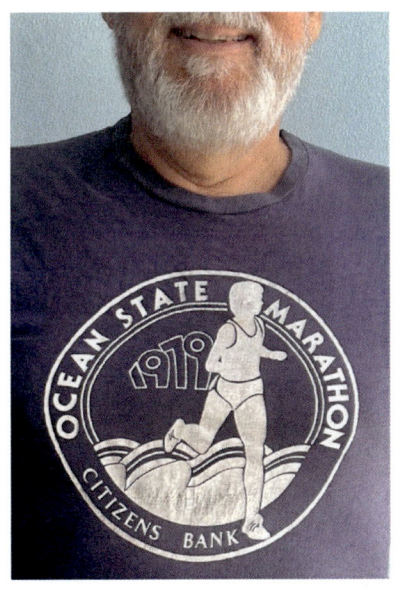

Newport, Rhode Island, November 4, 1979—photo: July 2022

TAVISTOCK

in small and large groups
we studied our behavior
in the here-and-now

there's little to teach
that we could not discover
searching our own minds

our ids and egos
supplied all the rich, raw grist
needed for learning

the infrastructure
of large organizations
was found in our selves

we excavated
our collective unconscious
those long, deep weekends

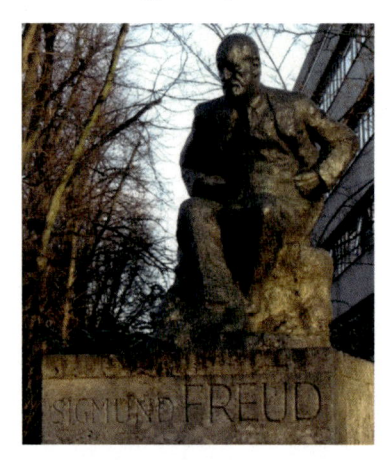

Annual Group Relations (Tavistock) conferences organized by The George Washington University in Longmeadow MA, 1979-1985

Photo: Statue of Sigmund Freud at the Tavistock Institute, London, England. Source: Wikipedia

BOB

we two young seekers
serendipitously met
five decades ago

we would change the world
ardent psych-fueled zealots
open skies beckoned

supportive duet
exchanging brilliant brainstorms
pollinating dreams

your maps showed real Earth
my mediation showed how
to reach common ground

careers now complete
in rear-view mirror I see
we grew each other

Bob Abramms and I supported each other's work through our early professional years (1980's)

BULGARIAN SHAKEDOWN

police came aboard
our overnight non-stop coach
—or so we'd been told

checking our passports
foreigners just passing through
"you have no visa!"

as if offended
"but you are in my country
without permission!"

"you must pay your fine
or I'll take you off this train"
"how much, sir?" I smiled

through window I watched
a man is taken away
I've wondered his fate

In Sofia, Bulgaria, with Trish enroute from Ljubljana, Slovenia, to Istanbul, Turkey, summer 1981. Photo: Sofia train station today (rail.cc)

WHAT DID PAUL BELIEVE?

with Trish in Izmir
met a history teacher
going to Efes

"may we tag along?"
bus driver dropped us nearby
we climbed a wire fence

walked through field of oats
no gate, no guards, no tourists
only we were there

Jeff gave us lectures
as we wandered fabled ruins
history awoke

when Saul of Tarsus
preached his gospel on this stage
what did he believe?

Trish "performing" at the amphitheater in Ephesus
(Efes), Turkey, Summer 1981

GROWING MTI

the sprout was struggling
headwinds battered her start-up
few thought it would work

needs more time, they said
credentials required, they said
not so, I believed

mediation works
just have the conversation,
with safeguards, I said

early adopters
made the sprout a sturdy tree
you proved me correct

dear trusty old friends
retired, but our bond remains
how can I thank you?

Bruce Newman and Ray Rusin, early adopters of Managerial Mediation from 1980's, now dear friends. Photo: July 2022, Westerly, Rhode Island

LANDING IN LENINGRAD

arrived on White Night
we expected a greeter
I don't speak Russian

sent by Moscow host
eager to meet next colleagues
no greeter showed up

"do. you. speak. English?"
I called out to airport crowd
helpers soon appeared

so, we found Masha
driving empty city streets
midnight's eerie dusk

her Stalin-esque home
no Cold War tensions found here
kind folks everywhere

With Masha and my daughter Su at Kirov ballet and opera theater, Leningrad (now St Petersburg), summer solstice, 1990

NIGHT TRAIN TO KIEV

we boarded early
settling into our couchette
a tap on our door

"you are in my room"
or something like, in Russian
my two-tongue reflex:

"¿ay, hay problema?"
(not English? — then the other)
he grinned in surprise

Cuban diplomat
found our one common language
wheels began rumbling

over bowls of borscht
a lucky conversation
through the night to Kiev

With daughter Su aboard overnight train from Moscow to Kiev. Photo taken by our new Cuban friend, June 1990

MY MIDLIFE CRISIS

life was pretty good
but not good enough, I feared
is this all there is?

I yanked up my roots
to transplant myself back home
rebooting my life

harder than I thought
tears blurred my westward vision
U-turn tempted fate

now, thirty years on
right choice, but poorly thought out
my foresight was dim

it's worked out, somehow
Lady Luck wed persistence
crisis got resolved

From Connecticut to Kansas, October 1991.
Photo: Circa 1990, Bloomfield, Connecticut

AN OLD FLAME

she reached across miles,
decades, and careers long past
an email surprise

our life-plans in flux
rescripted in middle age
by personals ad

we explored ourselves
with witty conversation
warming our shared space

our journeys diverged
seemed lost to forgotten times
then … my inbox rang

how are you, old friend?
I want to learn about you
and about myself

Mary Sue, early 1992, reconnected 2020. Photo undated

A BRIDGE IN CAIRO

a dad and daughter
houseguests of taxi-man's aunt
toured sights by day

small home packed nightly
curious neighbors dropped in
check out foreigners

young ones shared card games
Su's teen-girl celebrity
American myth

practicing English
"to where you go tomorrow?"
"Israel, by bus"

Ahmed's cautious smile
bridged the fraught chasm between us
"we like Palestine"

Photo: 1992

MANDELA

the air's electric
yesterday's election's done
Madiba has won!

apartheid is dead!
Blacks' dreams rise from deep despair
Whites hope for the best

my host is driving
campaign posters falling fast
from wooden light poles

"think I could take one?"
we stop quickly in the street
souvenir captured!

from above my desk
my political hero
speaks to me today

Durban, KwaZulu-Natal, South Africa, May 11, 1994. Photo 2021

PAPA SMURF

my five young charges
Lima, Nazca, Cuzco by
intercity bus

*hablo español
¿cuánto cuesta boleto?
¿hay baño cerca?*

guiding my small flock
through colorful *mercados*
on cobblestone streets

I'm called "Papa Smurf"
proud title for this old dad
swells my loving heart

back home, I received
this memorial statue
my prized possession

Peru, August 1995
Photo 2022: My daughter's gift has graced my desk since 1995

WE CHOSE TO HIKE

only half-way up
the bus is already there
Inca sun's burning

blisters start to bleed
no one thought to bring water
our legs are rubber

bounding far ahead
Quechuas jog with backpacks
coca in their cheeks

we rest on boulders
the ruins still not in sight
how bad could this get?

our plight demands grit
straining to rise to our feet
no choice, must slog on

Sean at Machu Picchu, Peru, August 1995. Photo by Su

EARTHQUAKE

wobbling and stumbling
through an archway's cool shadow
is this vertigo?

I knelt to not fall
others scream—it's not just me
must be an earthquake!

big waves in small pool
sloshing bathers side to side
frantic to climb out

I stood to see beach
is Banderas Bay still there?
tsunami coming?

a *temblor* for my
experience collection
the "big one," so far

Puerto Vallarta, Colima–Jalisco earthquake, 9 October 1995, 9:35 am
Photo: Los Tules Resort, scene of the earthquake experience

HOW MTI GOT ITS WEBSITE

I'm falling behind
last guy without a website
tech is marching on

renting mailing lists,
printing flyers, licking stamps
—buggy-whip business!

poured another cup
at Sunday's breakfast table
where to go from here?

the best sites are taken
I need a home on the web
think outside the box!

triple entendre:
"mediationworks" dot com
holy eureka!

mti | MEDIATION TRAINING INSTITUTE

At home with Susan in Prairie Village, Kansas, 1996
MTI's website and its contents were acquired by Eckerd College in 2012

THE BRIEF VOYAGE OF *RESOLVE*

the *Resolve* set sail
from a suburb in Kansas,
an ill-conceived launch

grossly unprepared,
she ran out of provisions
at the boarding dock

her novice skipper's
charts did not show rocky cays
lurking 'neath her hull

savvy reporters
saw Captain Dan's naiveté,
predicted shipwreck

Resolve sunk promptly,
but a treasure was salvaged:
"never sail again"

DANA for Congress
www.mediationworks.com

I was a candidate for the U.S. House of Representatives from the third district of Kansas, 1998—"The first non-adversarial campaign in the history of politics" whose slogan was "Put a mediator in the House." Lost primary to Dennis Moore, who won the general election in November.

9/11

my sister called me
"are you watching TV now?"
"no, I'm at my desk"

he is at his desk
North Tower, floor ninety-six
first one to see it

he stands, stares, transfixed
the speck is growing larger
"what the hell is that?"

now, others see it
someone screams, "is that a plane?"
all jump up, look out

others try to duck
his eyes open 'til it strikes
wants to see The End

September 11, 2001, 8:46:40 am (7:46.40 in Prairie Village, Kansas)
Photo credit: CNN (second plane hitting South Tower)

WHAT OF ME IS YOU?

we gathered one day
Gant-side cousins in one place
a rare reunion

years have grown us up
grandkids of Katherine and Guy
death lurks our cohort

Midwest country stock
our shared genes sum twelve percent
nature-nurture blend

from these common roots
our branches have spread afar
distant twigs lose touch

I stand in wonder
what parts of me are in you?
what of you is me?

Summer 2003, Rayville, Missouri
First cousins, from left: Lonnie, Deana, John, Kay Jon, Sheila, Bob, Liz, Dan, Delores, Dennis. Not present: J.K.'s Jim, Randy's family

MILE HIGH

approaching Mile High
we have all come, our hearts thrill
to see Obama

giddy faces glow
hope and change feel within reach
in rainbow skin tones

sixty thousand friends
congratulating ourselves
trust is in the air

my spine tingles as
his family walks on stage
folks like us, they seem

but dreams have been crushed
enemies of the people
have won the race war*

Obama's acceptance speech, Denver's Mile High stadium, 28 August 2008

_____

* So it seems in July 2022

DEDICATION

you can't comprehend
how precious you are to me
I was your age, once

filled with future's dreams:
goals, adventures, loves, hatchlings(?)
yet to be made real

Nan felt what I feel
reaching out, yet holding back
her love ached, like mine

I watch from afar
your special stars beckon you
you're on your journey

you're Papi's vectors
to future's remnants of me
this book is for you

Dedication for *Haiku Quintets,* published 2021
Photo: Puerto Vallarta, 2010

BIG GUY

"wait for the big guy"
the hike leader told our troop
I glanced back … who's that?

morning mist-slick trail
day-trek through Alaskan pines
up steepening path

we brought up the rear
youthful speedsters raced ahead
we're aging strollers

breathless, we catch up
rested, they're eager to go
our troop's out of sync

"you okay, big guy?"
I am Jon's little brother
I'm not a "big guy"

Sitka, Alaska, July 2010, with Susan
Image source: pixels (2019 photo, the same trail referenced in this haiku

MY PAKISTANI SEATMATE

seemed a nice fellow
engineer from Karachi
back home to visit

he sought to teach me
while captive on this long flight
nine-eleven's truth:

*"you must understand
Zionist conspiracy
to hate all Muslims"*

I listened with care
sincere views of a smart man
mired in crazy myth

not so different
from others that come to mind
we deplaned with tact

Aboard non-stop flight from Chicago to Istanbul, September 3, 2011
Image source: ancient-symbols

HANOI HAIRCUT

the sidewalk barber
invited this old GI
had we been foes, once?

his improvised shop
mirror hanging on the wall
with tools of his trade

cyclos streaming by
narrow street's pedal traffic
amused riders watched

fifty years ago
beyond my imagining
"wow! I'm in the North"

he did a good job
his paltry fee's not enough
—hundred percent tip

Hanoi, Vietnam, 3 May 2015

PITCH TALES

our family game
every Dana and Hendrix
had to learn to play

each new baby served
as table's next centerpiece
to pass cards around

Duncan shot the moon
through Granddaddy's cigar smoke
with no trump to lead[*]

Nannie's shy bidding
Lowell's odd dealing logic
Jon's intrepid play

we laughed 'til we ached
decades of witty banter
cemented our bond

At Deana's house in 2016, just one generational snapshot since the1950's. From left: Su, Seamus, Claribel, Jon, Deana, Dan, Lowell. Photo by Susan

---

[*] Circa 1960

ICEBERG

my head whipped around
rifle-shot sound cracked the air
echoes of echoes

morning quiet's rocked
two house-size chunks rolled over
roiling the gray sea

a small tsunami
splashed clunking stones at my feet
stirring salty smells

pregnant icebergs speak
Inuits know by their shape
when a birth is due

locals paid no heed
nothing to see here, it seemed
just avoid the shore

The subject iceberg moments before it split with a bang
Qaqortoq, Greenland, September 1, 2016, 10:05 am

THE PICKPOCKETS

"bird poop" dropped on me
walking under leafy trees
it looked very real

immediately
two kind señoras appeared
pointing overhead

they wiped off my shirt
one in front and one behind
they worked so quickly!

then, just as quickly
they hopped in a passing car
my, how convenient!

thanking them, I found
my under-shirt pouch unzipped
those gals knew their tricks

Buenos Aires (Palermo), Argentina, February 2017
Photo credit: Essential Destinations

THE GREAT AMERICAN ECLIPSE

once in a lifetime
we gathered in Sister's yard
my grandkids flew in

dusk overcame us
special sunglasses in place
cows went to their barn

corona's ring shone
"oooooo! wow! awesome! holy cow!"
was all we could say

nightfall in daytime
what did our ancestors think
without the science?

two minutes later
confused cows returned to graze
wondered "what the eff?"

Near Millville, Missouri, 21 August 2017, 1:21 pm

ESCAPING SAIGON

"are these seats taken?"
thus began conversation
we told our stories:

*as Saigon collapsed
he was Nguyen Cao Ky's pilot
to a U.S. ship*[*]

*she came with three kids
among the last to escape
on later chopper*

*a sailor saved them
son vowed to thank him, when grown
their lives hung by threads*

two rapt hours later
we bid them, "have a good day"
my story was brief

Aboard Seattle-to-Sydney cruise, October 16, 2017
Newspaper photo of the mom, her kids, and the sailor

---

[*] USS Blue Ridge, April 30, 1975

SARUNI

our dear Maasai friend
animal interpreter
Serengeti whiz

knows wild's secret ways
mother died by buffalo
his shield is savvy

Superman's eyesight
hippo, elephant, giraffe,
lion whisperer

he seeks two more wives
anglophone guide who can drive
may be chief some day

saw Nairobi once
"why would anyone live there?"
home is paradise

Saruni and friends, Maasai Mara, Kenya, August 2018

PUERTO VALLARTA

Mexican home town
gem of the Pacific side
warm air, warm people

relaxed or rowdy
choices galore, pick your style
Banderas playground

malecón strollers
buskers, artists, vendors vend
stone-stackers stack stones

palo volador
deft gravity-defiers
I'll just watch, thank you

zona 'mantica
gays and straights happily share
phobes might just stay home

since Richard and Liz
flocking snowbirds come to roost
"I just love this place!"

Photo: February 2019. We stayed in PV for up to three months most winters until pandemic struck in 2020

SUNSET

masts pierce sunset's glare
my bay shimmers and glimmers
night-time coming soon

perfect wavelengths blend
reflecting sky and water
photons touch my eye

uncorking my mind
music's harmonies give voice
to my struggling heart

colors morph slowly
cotton clouds keeping close watch
day's sun all gone now

dark descends in haste
sun's light fades, my pen is blind
last haiku tonight

Photo: 19 September 2019 from our west window in Sarasota. This is my first haiku quintet and the sunset that inspired it. In the three years since, I have written over 300 more, including all contained in this memoir.

MY NIGERIAN ATHEIST FRIEND

half a world away
my neighbor in cyberspace
he must hide his truth

wife, friends, family
die-hard zealots of dogma
religionists all

God's set men seek wealth
streets littered with loud churches
monstrous billboards shout

so many pastors
shrilling mindboggling song-sprees
launch zombie-like trance

African dark zone
be careful, my new-found friend
your brave words give hope

Composed 16 December 2019. He reached out to me after reading my e-book *The Reason Revolution*. Most words above are lifted from his emails to me. He's the poet. I am his haiku arranger. Image is a generic silhouette, not his likeness. He must remain anonymous for his safety.

SUPERBOWL 2020

some haiku snapshots
in case you missed the big game
Chiefs beat SFO

fifty-year drought ends
comeback kid, passing maestro
MVP Mahomes

Hard Rock's sea of red
half-time: J-Lo, Shakira
Reid's Gatorade dunk

ads more fun than game
Bloomberg's ten million bucks … poof!
take breaks during play

KC wild tonight
so sorry, San Francisco
oh well, there's next year

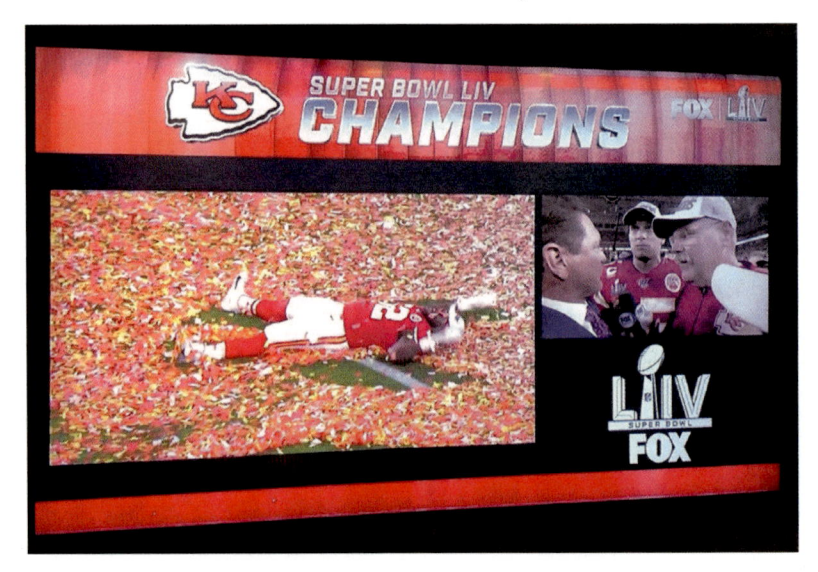

TV screenshot 2 February 2020. I am not a sports fan, but we watched this special game while in Puerto Vallarta. KC was once our home.

JOURNEY OF A WHITE LIBERAL

I thought I was clear
black sheep from White upbringing
have I been redeemed?

Woodstock, Africa
wept at *Uncle Tom's Cabin*
own my privilege

Floyd's murder by knee
Breonna killed while she slept
Brunswick jogger shot

Black voices stirred me
Black history haunted me
Blacks' burden crushed me

racism's stain laid bare
justice-shattering newsflash
shook me to my core

Composed 29 August 2020 as the afterword for my e-book, *Common Ground: Haiku, Mediation, and Police Reform*. Image source: CNN.com

2020

existential year
pressing us to glean meaning
from its stark darkness

a pinhole of life
lush verdant complexity
one glimpse at a time

unmask hidden joys
in the leaded gray cloudscape
of collective grief

find strength or perish
trust Blind Instinct to survive
like Victor Frankl

Covid's simple quiz
each day's choice to live or die
I'll say *Yes to Life*

Composed 24 October 2020. Inspired by Frankl's writings on logotherapy.
Photo: Victor Frankl revisiting Auschwitz. Source: Victor Frankl Institute, Vienna

AGING IN QUARANTINE

yep, been there, done that
bucket list mostly checked off
one hell of a ride

to-do list is done
my book is eight decades thick
awesome read, so far

golden years rush by
then is gone, but now is sweet
quarantine cocoon

young folks' dreams burn bright
time's a-wastin', boredom screams
fear of missing out

old man's few coins left
young man's wealth cries for splurging
I've plenty to last

Dan Dana

Feminist

Husband & Father Of Strong Women

Composed 14 November 2020. Image: Name tag at breastfeeding conference attended with wife and daughter, Washington DC, circa 2003

JANUARY 6

reciting haiku
zoom with my humanist friends
a normal Wednesday

CNN on mute
ominous morning headlines
what's the Breaking News?

Trump's mob storms the steps
smashing capitol's windows
Proud Boys shout MAGA

we quit zoom to watch
glued to news for hours and months
will his slow coup work?

thick dread fills this room
dying dream's sickening stench
hard to breathe in here

Composed 6 January 2021. Photo source: CNN

COVID CHICKS

locked down in home jail
virus-tethered, time to spare
why not hatch some chicks?

high-rise condo perch
not your grandpa's chicken ranch
fitting view for fowl

rooster's dad-deed done
delivered by Fedex stork
don't scramble these eggs!

three weeks 'til hatch-day
incubator surrogate
warms and turns her kids

pecks and chirps announce
freedom from shell confinement
set to fly the coop!

Composed 14 January 2021. Photo: Day four of life on the outside

PEDICURE BOBBI

my monthly friend
my happy toes' hottest date
my feet's indulgence

my daughter's cohort
mom of kids of like ages
as my two grand-ones

your listening ear
calls forth tales of younger years
buried in time's dust

your wide-open mind
invites my odd flavorings
of life's smorgasbord

our calendared chats
stir this Papi's yearning for
Covid's hostages

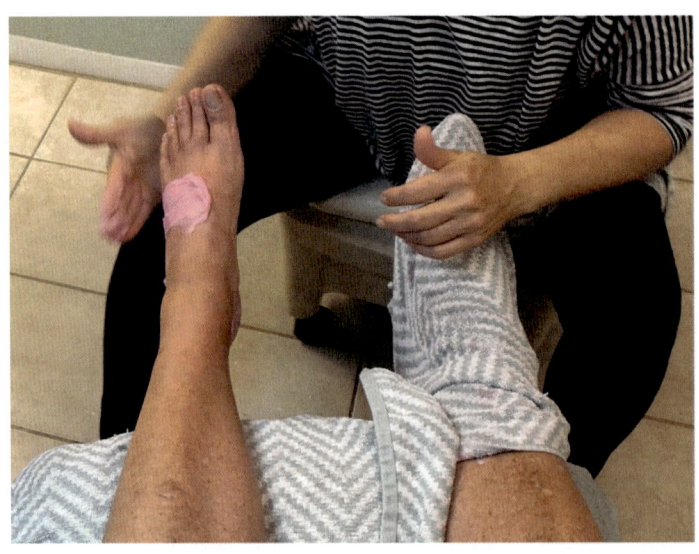

Composed 16 February 2021. I have been seeing "Pedicure Bobbi" for the past two years (as of July 2022).

IN YOUR HANDS NOW

here's Martin, my gem
we've made gorgeous harmony
since my Woodstock year

picking and strumming
with friends and in reverie
my hands shaped her sound

your deft touch will form
next half-century's moments
you're her new escort

in groups and solo
you'll make magic together
long beyond my years

what a trip we've shared!
Seamus, take this worn baton,
she's in your hands now

Composed 1 April 2021 as I gifted my Martin D-28 (owned since 1969) for Seamus's 21st birthday. Photos: 2000 and 2021 (same guitar in different light)

FRESH START CAFÉ

by haiku or prose
we Scribes of many flavors
flee our covid caves

quiet, shady brunch
clever, savory menu
—pure Sarasota!

our neighborhood spot
for unrushed conversation,
downtown's hidden gem

balmy day's fresh start,
twice-jabbed nearby denizens
munch our lunch mask-free

tell no one but friends:
six-thirty south orange ave,
please keep our secret!

Scribes, a Sarasota writers' group, at brunch, 30 May 2021

SOAR, CLARIBEL, SOAR!

our clan's loved fledgling,
eager eagle set to fly,
your world awaits you

your wings will lift you
to wuthering distant heights
beyond now's knowing

your mind will be blown,
your horizons will recede,
your wisdom will surge

you'll meet sage teachers,
life-school's diverse faculty:
people unlike you

launch your journey with
this ticket to anywhere
—soar, Claribel, soar!

Composed 6 June 2021, graduation gift. Image credit: Dad's Productions

Restrictions and limitations:

1. Effective date: 6 June 2021
2. Expiration: One year after ticket holder's graduation from college
3. Destination limited to surface of planet Earth. Ticket not yet valid for interplanetary travel.

A TREE OF WONDER

thirty years ago
I planted seeds in Moscow
now, I'm wondering …

how did they first sprout?
who kept them fed and watered?
did a forest grow?

were conflicts resolved?
were relationships repaired?
did they talk it out?

Russians read my words
in a language I don't know
their minds thought my thoughts

at long last I've found
a sapling in Cold War's land
a tree of wonder

Composed 16 September 2021, the day I first received a photo of the Russian edition of my 1988 book, *Managing Differences* (translation: "Overcoming Disagreements"), held by a friend in Latvia.

PAPER TRAIL

I hope to preserve
this Papi's love-crafted words
on holiday cards

haiku memories
rescued from Yule's common fate:
Christmas morning's trash

shredded red ribbons
and crumpled wrapping paper
shall not be their grave:

beloved gap year girl,
seems you've caught the travel bug,
a healthy virus

our own tech wizard
who can see under the hood
of our devices

Composed 13 December 2021, back-up to haiku in holiday cards to Claribel (fourth stanza) and Seamus (fifth stanza)

BIGOTED GOATS

poor little Greta
is it her ears, or her breed?
she is an outcast

Blossom's kin shun her
blocking her from the haystack
with selfish head-butts

Blossom's clan snuggles
to warm against winter's chill
Greta sleeps alone

Greta's LaMancha
Blossom's Nigerian Dwarf
unlike visages

are goats bigoted?
surely not my dear grandkids!
they were raised with love

Composed 25 January 2022. Photo: Holding one of my Nigerian Dwarf grandkids at the Connor mini-farm near Woodstock, Connecticut, 2016

WATCHING WAR BEGIN

we stand on the bank
of Ukraine's river of blood
awaiting Putin

his fragile ego
breeds deranged lust to rebuild
Soviet empire

at what human cost?
horrific suffering pays
toxic hubris' toll

did the sweet scent of
the Orange Revolution
merely stay this stench?

shall evil prevail?
today we know fate's answer
watching war begin

CNN screen, minutes after Russia launched attack, 23 January 2022

THE SWING

the little Black boy
walked with his mom on the path
in front of my swing

he gazed longingly
I looked up from my reading
brown eyes met blue eyes

we each understood
this instant in history
through our race's lens

standing, I gestured
"would you like to have the swing?"
Mom smiled *"thank you, sir"*

one more grain of sand
to resist racism's vile tide
—White men can be kind

The swing where it happened, Bayfront Park, Sarasota, 9 March 2022

MY LAST HIKE

no bones were broken
just bloody scrapes and bruises
face down in red dust

loose sand on steep rocks
my aging reflexes lagged
as if paralyzed

close calls teach lessons
averted catastrophes
draw one's attention

my youth's carelessness
fading to old man's caution
fragile future's risk

I've had my fair share
good luck's limited supply
I'll hike flatter trails

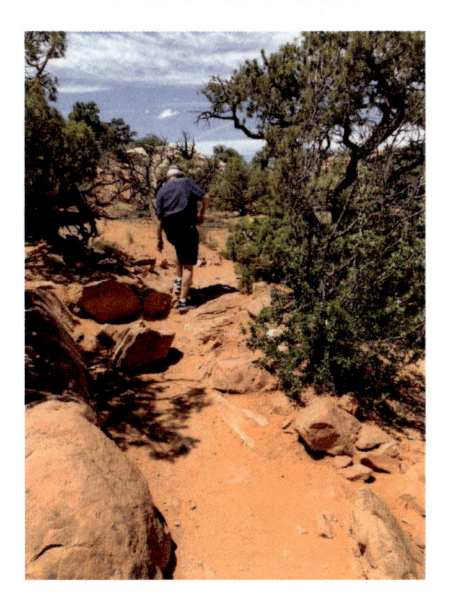

Composed 13 May 2022. Photo by Susan 10 minutes before my crash in Canyonlands NP, Moab, Utah

MORMONS

Mormons are nice folks
sister-missionary pairs
strolling Temple Square

one week in Salt Lake
no scientific study
just first impression

every smiling face
tells us "you are welcome here"
scripted care still works

courtesy abounds
even drivers are polite
no rude honks or shouts

Mormons are nice folks
like secular humanists
but with religion

Susan with a pair of sister-missionaries, Temple Square, Salt Lake City, 19 May 2022

WE GOT COVID

dodged virus 'til now
tested positive today
Susan got it first

we thought we were safe
twice jabbed and twice boosted, but
Omicron broke through

mild symptoms so far:
just sniffling, sneezing, coughing
—and quarantining

no worries, dear friends
dying is not on our chart
we're old, but healthy

just one more fun bit
tossed in this memory box,
for grandkids' grandkids

Composed 13 June 2022

SMORGASBORD OF THE MIND

scribes brunch together
authors, novelists, poets,
the odd haikuist

word-nerd gathering
careers done, brains still cooking
write, read, talk, repeat

scribblers serve their dish
steamed, grilled, poached, stir-fried, half-baked
twice-monthly mind-snacks

word salad welcome
creativity simmers
in scriveners' kitchens

nourishing munchies
our smorgasbord of the mind
a writers' pub crawl

Lakewood Ranch (Florida) Scribes admiring a table-full of our creations, led by Aroon Chaddha (center above), 25 June 2022

ANCESTRAL CAVE

on this very spot
two thousand generations
stood here before me

smoke from your fire pits
still blacken this cave's ceiling,
preserving remains

babies were born here
children played with rustic toys
old, injured, sick died

each life's like the last
through unfathomed far-future
my genes contain you

I flew above clouds
on a silver eagle's wings
to reach back to you

Cave near Pont du Gard in southern France inhabited by ancestral hominids for 600,000 years, including interbred Homo sapiens and Neanderthals from 40,000 years ago.
Photo: 8 September 2022

STRUTHOF

she flies overhead
in dove's feathered innocence
at a safe remove

watching "pieces" crawl
up icy steps for roll call,
then falter and die

smelling stench of death,
of their shit, of rotting flesh,
of chimney's vile fumes

these are my own kind
"Honor and Homeland" calls us
to fight senseless wars

no dove's innocence;
nationalism is poison,
humanity's curse

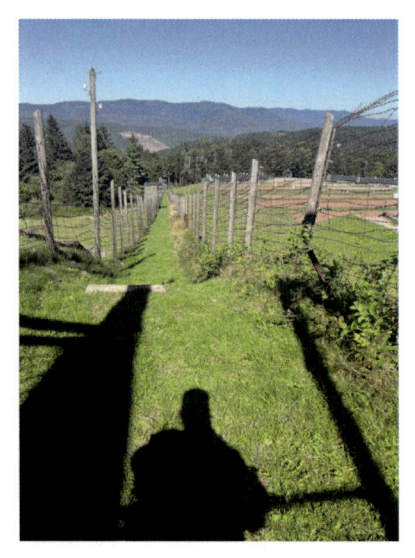

Photo 22 September 2022: Shadow selfie between double barbed wire fence surrounding prison where 22,000 victims of nationalism died 1941-1944, Natzwiller-Struthof, Nazi-occupied France

HURRICANE IAN

we'd been gone a month
Ian chose to come visit
such awkward timing!

on collision course
we'd hoped to land before him
nay, quoth weather gods

stranded near Dulles
while he wreaked windy havoc
we watched helplessly

he didn't stay long
but left a trash heap behind
a most thoughtless guest!

so that's my story
a final haiku quintet
to end this memoir

AccuWeather screenshot 28 September 2022. Hurricane Ian struck near Sarasota the same day we were scheduled to return from France. Our condo was undamaged.

NOW

wishing there were words
to meet this morning's moment,
to preserve its truth

pelicans diving
for breakfast of chilled herring,
starting their day, too

blue herons flying
to their daily hideaway,
knowing their way back

our world is spinning,
giving us this fine morning,
moon's nightshift is done

this eternal now
cannot be captured and kept
for there are no words

Full moon setting over Sarasota Bay, 18 March 2022, 8:00 am
Although this life-snippet was composed earlier, it is always "now"

2
SUSAN

I would not attempt to illustrate this remarkable woman in grayscale—her exquisite being defies plainly descriptive language. The medium of poetry allows me to paint her in more beguiling colors.

SONG FOR SUSAN

dear co-traveler,
this path we chose together
hand in hand we go

your innate kindness
guiding me and growing me
showing me myself

our trust locks our bond
no dark suspicions intrude
e duo unum

plain humanism
no supernatural myth
we believe in us

onward 'til our end
living day by precious day
my friend, love, heart, mate

Photo: our wedding, 1 July 2000

FINDING HER

like ripening fruit
he was growing more ready
to re-pair his life

he'd relived a time
he had never lived before
only imagined

wiser choice this time
having learned the recipe
of love's secret sauce

armed with his treatise
he sallied Cupid's broad plain
vision in focus

his arrow struck gold
two puppies snug in our box
'til death we'll remain

We met in 1995, married in 2000
Photo: Lofoten, Norway, June 2019

THE WRONG SUSAN

"good morning, Susan,
I've landed in Miami"
she paused, seemed confused

it was a long flight
my reminder notes got mixed
"sorry, my mistake"

I owed her a call
back home, I apologized
I blew it, I thought

not the jealous type
one of her fine qualities,
partner-type, for me

retired together
in our condo by the bay
she's the right Susan

Setting: Miami International Airport, August 25, 1995, ~ 5:00 am
Photo: At home in Sarasota, 2019

MY VALENTINE

there's mojo in two
one eye's not enough, nor ear
one leg cannot stand

one heart's not enough
mine hardly beats without you
my self's other half

one plus one is three
in love's odd mathematics
our equation works

one half-life's too short
I have doubled-down on you
a winning wager

mi Valentina
you are twice the worth of me
with you, I am whole

Composed Valentine's Day, 2021
Caricature by Sean Connor, 2000

ANGEL ON EARTH

no spirit-elf myth
if angels on earth there be
I know one quite well

foresees others' wants
nurse-caregiver at her core
off-scale thoughtfulness

nurtures by nature
needy children's advocate
voice-and-choice's champ

tenacious pit bull
restores sundered families
mama-bear fierceness

makes our house a home
kindest person ever known
I kiss her nightly

Photo: The angel in 1953

BON VOYAGE

we're a cruising team
crossing fierce Pandemic Sea
each other's first mate

rising every morn
navigating through each day
'til our goodnight kiss

we share the tiller
steering clear of rocky shoals
and Covid's dark reef

yon fog-shrouded shore
who can see this journey's end?
we bid bon voyage

dear co-traveler
quarantine's sweet companion
let's sail on, my love

Composed as dedication for *Songs of the Pandemic*
Photo: Greenland, August 2016

PUPPIES IN A BOX

it's often declared
among relationshipped folk:
"marriage is hard work"

not so, in our nest
I don't own you, nor you me
we are more than two

no promises bind
I choose you afresh each day
our freedom's unchained

kindnesses gifted
each in debt to the other
we're each the winner

primal friendship, the
simple secret sauce known by
puppies in a box

Image source: wallpaperplay

HOW TO MAKE LOVE

no deep secret here
simple truth for keen partners
use this power tool:

pay close attention
mate's small bids for connection
accept, don't reject

turn toward, not away
turn-aways kill trust, troth, love
turn-towards cement bond

listen when she speaks
applaud her career success
laugh at her fun pun

meet kiss-hint with yours
subtle gestures flow both ways
turning toward makes love

Photo: Walk-bridge at home of Elizabeth Taylor, Puerto Vallarta

MICROECONOMICS OF LOVE

fairness your focus?
getting less than you're giving?
wrong frame for true love!

keep score = self-defeat
tally win-lose = ensure loss
bean-counters divorce

one plus one is three
giving yields rich abundance
re-think common sense

transactional love?
oxymoron can't compute
quid pro quo cheats both

frank talk is core task
caring truth is love's tonic
surrender control

Photo: Belgium, 2008

THREE MAGIC WORDS

practiced life-partners
know well I-Love-You's effect
when sincerely voiced

triggers like response
reciprocity's reflex
ripens love's sweet taste

less known and practiced
three more magic power-words
each toolbox should hold

when disputes erupt
blame, fault, anger take the wheel
drives us in a ditch

harness that reflex
take high road to love's repair
asking, Tell-Me-More

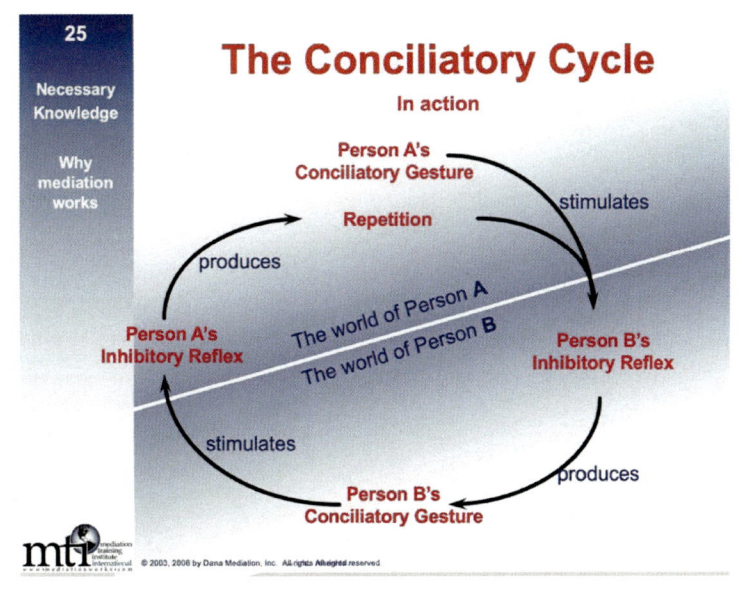

PowerPoint slide from MTI's mediation training course
Source: mediationworks.com

INEXPRESSIBLE

in one precious frame,
the three women I love most
my heart's joy I'll tell

this measly haiku
struggles to carry the freight
of love's sundry forms

too few syllables,
my thin thesaurus falls short
surely there's a way!

for want of language,
all who burst with love's heartbeat
wear this poet's shoes

inexpressible
in words known to humankind
d'ya know what I mean?

Susan, Claribel, and Su in Woodstock Valley, Connecticut, June 2021

KISSING QUANDARY

so snug on the couch
blanket tucked under your chin
blonde wisps frame your face

your afternoon nap
this precious at-home Sunday,
you've been working hard

sweet love swells my heart,
we're two puppies in a box
sharing life's comforts

might I sneak a kiss
on your cheek, but not wake you?
my lips want your warmth

no, you need this rest
you would lift your sleepy head
to greet my sly kiss

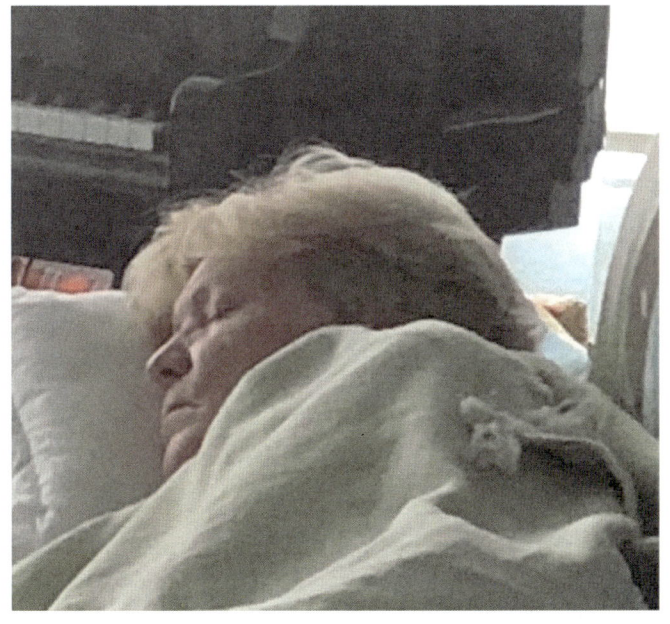

Photo taken from my desk while writing this haiku

DANCING QUEEN

ABBA's lively tune
brings forth a dazzling pixie
a spirit unleashed

her standard request
at cruise ships' midnight parties
and anyplace else

arms wave overhead
sparkling eyes, rapturous smile
her inner sprite glows

a gogo dancer
she coulda been a Rockette
or ballerina

standing here in awe
I'm her stiff, artless partner
she's my Dancing Queen

Photo: At her granddaughter's wedding, 5 August 2022

SUSAN'S NOT DONE YET

morning's alarm sounds
wake me at eight, you had asked
"I am not done yet"

did you finish it?
audiobook on your walk
"I am not done yet"

bacon on your plate,
I eye it with interest
"I am not done yet"

birthdays piling up,
stack getting fretfully high
"I am not done yet"

my idle question,
do you still love me, my Dear?
"I am not done yet"

SUSAN'S FAMILY

seven Moore cousins
Grandma's and Grandpa's treasures
formed their Kansas clan

from seventy-two
seven years of pregnancy
brought forth seven lives

three loyal sisters
new moms chasing girlhood dreams
filled with love and hope

heartland family
each one's future seemed secure
but three became two

lives, loves, losses borne
spanning time, miles, broken hearts
seven became six

Photo: All children of the Moore sisters, 1984

MY DREAM

she died in the night
I nudge her lifeless body
in bed beside me

her skin has grown cool
was she aware of dying?
did she not suffer?

panic engulfs me
what will life be without her?
dreadful thoughts rush in

what do I do now?
crushing grief clenches my heart
I'm lost and afraid

I startle awake
teary, I touch her warm skin
she stirs, "what's wrong, Sweets?"

ONLY A MOTHER CAN KNOW

her soul-crushing loss
secreted behind a veil
of smiling good cheer

grief's smothering shroud
cloaks her tomb of living death
no gladness can pierce

some few know her pain
mothers' tear-drenched lost-child club
woe to those who join

pin-hole view between
our safe home and lucky life,
her dark lonely cave

despair's icy grip
can't endure but can't move on
none but moms can know

Photo: Tyghe's foot molds in bronze

JUST YOU AND ME

for nine loving months
before birthing, sharing you
with the waiting world
                        it was just you and me

I nursed you to life
I fiercely held you to me
I protected you

now you're gone, so gone
lost to my sore, sobbing soul
no soft skin to sooth

none knew you like me
none loved like I loved you
no one cared like me

my mother-love aches
you remain inside me still
a hole in my heart
                        again, it's just you and me

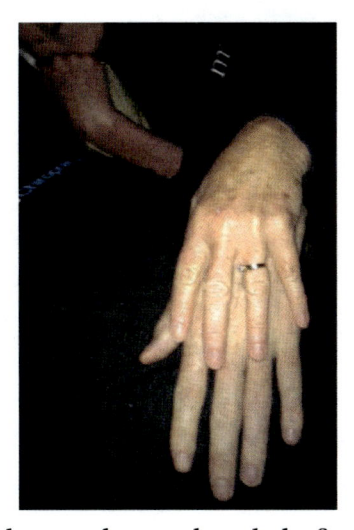

Photo: Mother and son, shortly before his death
Susan's reality through Dan's words

REUNION

four hard years have passed
I saw love in your sad eyes,
and you in mine

discovering now
Nana's back, I was not gone
my love did not lapse

stunned tears tell your grief
clever girl, but truth withheld
I now reappear

may joy now resume?
may years of needless sorrow
now fade behind us?

our searching eyes meet
how can the door be unlocked?
we don't hold the key

Photo: 26 September 2019, 8:15 pm, Olathe, Kansas

SURRENDER, MOVE ON

the good fight is lost
what should have been cannot be
just more needless hurt

mother's fierce duties
intending love and shelter
gaslit in darkness

toxic puppeteer
psychic danger found too late
poisoned soft young minds

how could I have seen
unforeseeable outcomes?
the damage is done

I've done all I can
now, accept futility
surrender, move on

Susan and her boys in 1983

SKIN THERAPY

grief overwhelms you
no good answers can be found
no words sooth your pain

can nothing be done?
am I helpless to help you?
must you just endure?

skin therapy heals
we lie together naked
skin-to-skin-to-skin

my skin feeds your skin
you absorb love through your pores
no talk, no action

our bodies soaking
in pure animal essence
therapeutic balm

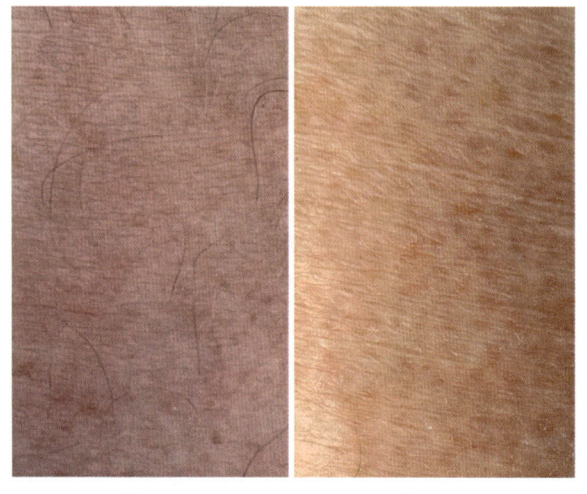

Dan   Susan
Patches of skin that often touch each other, communicating somehow

RESILIENCE

you are kind, thoughtful,
and generous to a fault
you are an angel

we who know you best
who return your love with love
are the lucky ones

strangers who stumble
into your warm sunshine are
stunned by your goodness

but those who squander
who trample your sweet kindness
discard your precious gifts

your softness is strength
you can rally from setback
you're resilient

3
ROOTS

Bayfront Park, Sarasota

IMMIGRANT ROOTS:

My earliest American ancestors immigrated from England in the decades following 1620. All lived full, eventful lives, about which I know nothing except dates and locations of their births and deaths. Below is a selection of people who were born in Europe and died in America and whose DNA I carry. Last is a native forefather who links me to the people who first populated the Western Hemisphere over 15,000 years ago.

The mission of this memoir is to capture some snippets of my own lived experience between those date markers in case some future descendant may wonder what happened in my world and time.

Immigrants on my father's side:

- Richard Dana (6th great-grandfather), 1617-1690, b. Manchester, England, d. Cambridge, Massachusetts
- Ann Holyoke (7th great-grandmother), 1620-1665, b. Warwickshire, England, d. Salem, Massachusetts
- Elizabeth Bancroft (8th great-grandmother), 1626-1711, b. Norwich, England, d. Lynn, Massachusetts
- Richard Warren (10th great-grandfather), 1585-1628, arrived aboard the *Mayflower*, December 21, 1620, b. Hertfordshire, England, d. Plymouth Colony, British Colonial America

Descendants' surnames include Dana, Brainard, Pratt, Stone, Bancroft, Holyoke, Warren, Buckminster, Gillis, Markham

Christina Brainard
grandmother

Alfred L. Dana
grandfather

Mary Bancroft
3d-great-grandmother

WESTPORT LANDING

we've arrived at last!
I'll soon leave this steamboat's deck
of stench and danger

by grace we've survived
may I never sail again
this blasted river!

days more by wagon
'til we start building our new
prairie home of sod

I shall not return
my kin stayed home, hereafter
known but by letter

seizing this moment
what will my grandchildren know
of my great journey?

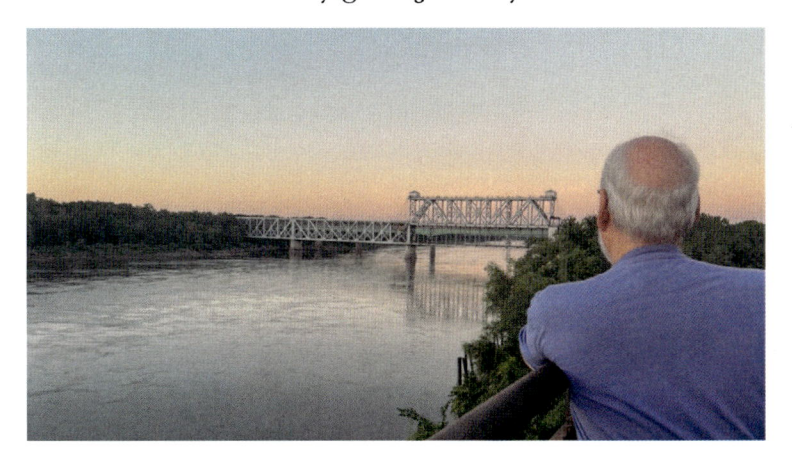

Gazing downstream at Westport Landing, Kansas City, August 10, 2022, the site where my teenage grandfather Alfred Luther Dana arrived in 1843 with his family from Marietta, Ohio, completing a months-long journey. Another week by wagon lay before them to their new homestead near Humboldt, Kansas, my father's birthplace, December 14, 1874.

Immigrants on my mother's side:

- Thomas Gant (7th great-grandfather), 1652-1721, b. Northamptonshire, England, d. Prince George, Virginia
- John Waller II (6th great-grandfather), 1673-1754, b. Buckinghamshire, England, d. Spotsylvania, Virginia
- Ellen Patterson (5th great-grandmother), 1707-1774, b. Dublin, Ireland, d. Berkeley, Virginia
- Powhatan (12th great-grandfather), 1545-1618 (Chief of Algonquin tribe in coastal Virginia, father of Pocahontas)

Descendants' surnames include Gant, Waller, Patterson, Hillyer, Grimes, Randolph, Kincaid, Robinson, Wyatt, Hanks

Emma Randolph
great-grandmother

James & Mary Gant
2d great-grandparents

Ludie Grimes
great-grandmother

Curiously, Susan and I discovered that we are 8th cousins once removed. Our most recent common ancestor was Sarah Elizabeth Mason (1670-1726) of Stafford, Virginia, who was my 8th great-grandmother and Susan's 7th great-grandmother.

The source of this information about my immigrant roots is the Family History Research Library, Salt Lake City, Utah, May 2022.

YOU CAME BEFORE

you have made me me
across centuries and seas
else, I would not be

each mating doubled
the rich depth of my gene pool
now, beyond measure

choices that you made
in England and Africa
gave me this one chance

my end could have come
but you survived lethal risks
forecasting my life

then, it was my turn
compelled so by Nature's laws
my root lengthens yours

Family History Library on Temple Square, Salt Lake City, 18 May 2022

VIKING ROOTS

According to DNA results from 23andme.com, I am 1.5% Scandinavian.

Am I a Viking?

Vikings ruled England
ruthless seaborne invaders
planting seeds and genes

English called them "Danes"
before Normans brought surnames
and standard spelling

what are my Norse roots?
"Dana" traced five hundred years
to medieval time

Danes changed history
by their bold expeditions
and seafaring ways

but my soft nature
seems less warlike Viking than
peaceful Norwegian

Photo: Viking Museum, Bøstad, Norway, 16 June 2019

NEANDERTHAL ROOTS:

According to DNA results from 23andme.com, I am 3% Neanderthal. All people alive today, except sub-Saharan Africans, share a similar percentage. This species of early human populated Europe from 400,000 to 40,000 years before present. They interbred on countless occasions with Homo sapiens from 100,000 YBP until their eventual extinction or absorption into the genome of modern humans, which amounts to about 60,000 years of coexistence. Assuming an average generational span of twenty years and allowing for multiple descendant lineages from a single Neanderthal ancestor, we of European ancestry could statistically have had billions of direct ancestors—an impossible number far beyond the peak Neanderthal population during that time, estimated at only 5000 to 50,000 individuals. So, you and I are direct descendants of several (perhaps all) Neanderthal individuals whose personal descendancy did not die out, including those who lived in the cave pictured here:

Photo: Grote Mandrin, one of many caves in France occupied intermittently by both Neanderthals and Homo Sapiens for thousands of years. Source: CNRS

Controversy surrounds the question of whether, or with what relative frequency, matings between Neanderthals and Homo sapiens were consensual. I depict two scenarios below representing the alternatives and leave it to science to find conclusive evidence to answer the question.

WE ARE NEANDERTHALS

(A consensual scenario)

early one evening
she was gathering firewood
not far from her cave

in nearby forest
a man—one of the Others—
hunted for squirrels

their young brown eyes met
gaze ignited yearning loins
in those guiltless times

some nine months later
Baby joined her shrinking clan
loved, as mothers do

my grandmother's love
three thousand lifespans ago
lives in me today

Image of a Neanderthal woman. Source: Earth Archives

WE ARE NEANDERTHALS

(A nonconsensual scenario)

early one evening
she was gathering firewood
not far from her cave

in nearby forest
a man—one of the Others—
hunted for squirrels

alone and helpless
her trusted kin did not hear
her faint anguished calls

such was the danger
when We and They encountered
in those lawless times

my grandmother's cries
three thousand lifespans ago
call to me today

The aggressors could have been, and no doubt were, of either species.

AFRICAN ROOTS

We Are African

Swahili greeting:
*Sisi ni watoto wa
Afrika ... jambo!**

grandmother left home
three thousand lifespans ago,
adventuring forth

inching around globe,
cave-steads lent safety from threats,
warm respite from harm

Eurocentric myth,
"invasive species" is us
who's the next "native"?

our bloodlines alloy,
we're all family, my friend
—African cousins

Image: Our grandmother (100,000 generations ago). Fossil reconstruction from likely period of the most recent common ancestor (concestor) of all humans alive today. Source: Houston Museum of Natural Science

---

* Translation: "We are all children of Africa ... hello!"

4
DEATH

Dan Dana
1945 September 23 – 20

Read my memoir
A Life Mostly Lived

My will instructs a gravestone with this inscription be placed with my ashes in Knoxville Cemetery, Ray County, Missouri.

The number of members of my contemporary extended family who remember my father as a living person can be counted on the fingers of one hand. A few elderly unrelated people who recall him, but who have less reason to do so, may still be standing among life's survivors. Soon, there will be none.

A Spanish phrase—"generación relevo"—helps visualize this passing. My sister Deana, brother Jon, and I are our parents' "relief generation"—picture a relay race where a runner takes the baton from the previous one, carrying it another leg onward. In this sense, our family lineage is a team, carrying forward our family history into the ever-receding future. This memoir is my turn at passing on our family's baton. I am endeavoring here to not drop it.

Harboring no supernaturalistic illusion that an afterlife may follow, I recognize that we are biology. Our place in the universe is cosmology. My life will term-out in a decade or two, if I'm lucky. Then, my own relief generation—Su, then Seamus and Claribel—will take their turns. My time aboard spaceship earth may be noted in the record only by birth date, death date, and a few sketchy details about what happened in-between.

Such paltry knowledge is all I have of the lives of my own ancestors of only a few generations ago. Their lived experiences ("life-snippets") died with them, and so are not knowable to anyone today. Prior to a few centuries ago, our ancestors' life-snippets—mine and yours—are lost forever. Yet, they lived full, interesting, busy lives every day, just like you and me, for hundreds, thousands, millions of years. Now it is our turn.

My intent and modest hope in compiling this memoir, in the year 2022, is to create a digital and physical document that may postpone the inevitable demise of all records of my existence. If successful, its contents will be known to my descendants for another generation or two. That's the most, it seems, that one can hope for without resorting to mysticism.

Meanwhile, as I imply in the poems below, I'm striving to make the most of my one shot at life.

AUTOBIOGRAPHY

I was born, I'll die
meanwhile, stuff is happening
this is no dry run

haiku tell my tale
snippets of chance, mind-glimpses,
snapshots of being

I'll live 'til I don't
in awe of my existence
mere speck in fate's scheme

this life will fade soon
descendants will know little
but my name and dates

must go "be here now"
thanks for your kind attention
I've got more to do

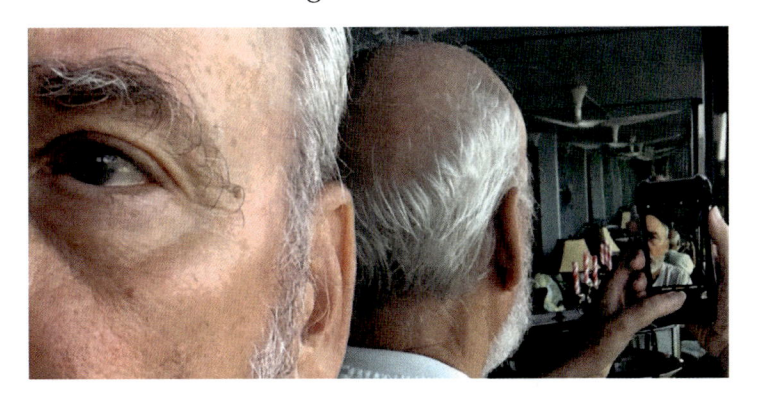

LIFE'S A MOVIE

what a show this is!
director's chair? – nah, just watch
seems almost real, eh?

laugh at comic bits
suspense—what'll happen next?
cry in tragic scenes

take a seat, my friend
relax, it's not about us
let's watch together

que será, será
whatever will be, will be
will be fun to see

far-future is known:
red sun will vaporize Earth
meanwhile, share popcorn

Inspired by comedian-philosopher George Carlin (1937-2008)
Image source: georgecarlin.com

WHAT IF?

counterfactual
ghosts lurk this reality,
shadows of what-if

who would "I" have been
if other sperm won the race
at my conception?

wife would not be mine,
daughter's, grandkids' lives unlived
who else might have been?

my choices have touched
those of myriad others
these tangled decades

alternate beings
died at the blind corner of
This or That

A choice-point in Bayfront Park, Sarasota

HAVE I MADE A DIFFERENCE?

most mortals hope to
leave the world a better place
as their exit nears

my career's true north
was teaching peacemaking skills
for both work and home

I often wonder
where and when those talking tools
made a difference

in lands I've not seen?
in languages I don't speak?
in lives not yet lived?

now, I write haiku
a frivolous enterprise
but maybe worthwhile?

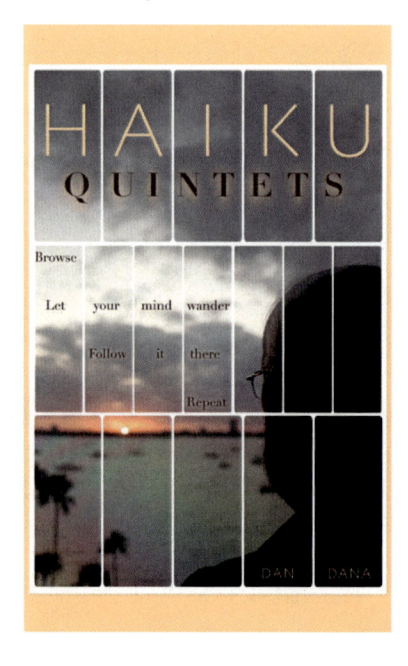

MY BUCKET LIST

yup, been there, done that
I have sailed Earth's seven seas
I've climbed Rockies' peaks

untold adventures
fill my memory neurons
life's been great—still is

old age marches on
contentment replaces thrill
pleasure's in small things

gazing on the bay
admiring other men's boats
glad they are not mine

pass time patiently
have meaningful fun each day
that's my bucket list

Photo: The haikuist at work

GOAT OR GEFN?

athletes and heroes
strive to wear that gilded crown:
<u>G</u>reatest <u>O</u>f <u>A</u>ll <u>T</u>ime

lust for fortune feeds
youthful pride's hungry soul while
I watch from afar

I've never summoned
enough fire in the belly
to climb pointless peaks

I'm competitive
about which of us is the
least competitive

as my race winds down
I'll wear my drab well-worn cap:
<u>G</u>ood <u>E</u>nough <u>F</u>or <u>N</u>ow

ALONG FOR THE RIDE

I'm a spectator
of world's unfolding drama
one unit of life

I'm not at the wheel,
just a wide-eyed passenger
hurtling through spacetime

on Earth's fragile skin
voyaging the vast unknown,
along for the ride

awash in deep awe
of this accidental trip
as long as it lasts

I'll binge on life's feast
with gratitude for blind luck
'til my final bite

Photo: Our home-hatched chick driving an unstrung 1972 Colombian tiple, rather like me

UNSPENT WEALTH

a lifetime of gems
assayed as worthless pebbles
can't take them with me

my elders' wisdom
gone to their final abyss
with their priceless wealth

young ones so busy
tending to vital concerns
as was I, back then

wishing I knew then
a smidge of what I know now
life's costly lessons

here, take these pebbles
this memoir of unspent wealth
my lifetime of gems

Photo 2016

TIME FLIES

days pass too quickly
each sweet moment should linger
if I had my way

bygone childhood wish:
"can't wait until tomorrow"
—tomorrow is now

hazy road ahead
my car seems stuck in high gear
near-sighted headlights

life's a one-meal deal
an exquisite cosmic feast
mystery salad

I'll savor each bite
my plate will be bare one day
so, dine with gusto

I HAVE SURVIVED, SOMEHOW

so many close calls
this seventy-six-year romp
lucky twists of fate

motorcycle crash
Honduran priests saved my butt
kept souvenir scars

year in Vietnam
hazy memories survive
pot smoker's Bronze Star

now, safely cocooned
in Sarasota treehouse
for the duration

few dangers ahead
except the one that kills me
… waiting … patiently

YOU ARE MY AFTERLIFE

my atoms will roam
join other earth-bound life forms:
mouse, bird, fish, worm, weed

as dad, my genes will
walk, talk, think, feel, reproduce
keeping human form

my molecules float
in air until Earth's days end
five billion years hence

Sun's sons go nova
generations of star-stuff
flung galaxy-wide

as teacher-writer
some wise bits may carry on
perhaps this haiku?

With Su, 1973   With Seamus, 2000

MISPLACED GRIEF

when I die, I'll cease
no missed bucket-list regrets
just pure nothingness

won't be me who grieves
you may mourn your loss of me,
a hole in your heart

our culture's last rite,
my funeral's not for me
I will not be there

celebrate my life
it's been a hell of a ride
then, get on with yours

I'll drink life's last drop,
but if the end's too bitter,
please pass the hemlock

With my life's sunset at a distant(?) horizon, I inscribe this non-mythologized view of end-of-life on a slate of haiku for my friends' comfort and other mortals' reflection.

JIM'S LAST GIFT

he reached out to me
final-exit day nearing
to bid me farewell

I admire him so
foresaw slippery slope's brink
drew clear-eyed courage

choice was his to make
appraised remaining time's worth
as is Reason's way

his life richly lived
left this world a better place
dignity enshrined

Jim's last gift to me:
priceless light on road ahead
thank you, my wise friend

Photo source: unknown

THAT GOOD NIGHT

quoth the young poet:
*"rage, rage against the dying
of the light"* – not yet!

myself, I think not
– I'll marvel in that moment,
what a trip I've had!

thankful for my mind,
thinking thoughts about this thought,
awesome cosmic gift

as life's process ends,
savoring final moments,
drifting into void,

I intend to go
"gentle into that good night"
I was here ... that's all

Photo: Dylan Thomas (1914-1953), source: Dylan Thomas Centre.
If I had faced death at age 39, I, too, may have raged.

REST IN PEACE

closer to life's end
than to its brash beginning
I watch world's demise

at an odd remove
as if from a mountaintop
through rose-colored lens

aaah, but you young ones
and those zillions yet to live
my heart bleeds, helpless

what will beset you?
what torment will you endure?
what fate will snare you?

meanwhile, life is good
I've lived in charmed time and place
I'm resting in peace

Overlooking Yosemite Valley from Columbia Rock, 2015

ON DYING

as life leaves this eye
what will I say to the world
on final exit?

to Mother Cosmos
returns borrowed molecules
deep thanks for the loan

such blind luck at birth!
fate has smiled kindly on me
vastly more than most

I'll live 'til I don't
the day unknowable yet
but I choose to choose

my life, not others'
when its end comes into view
it's mine to decide

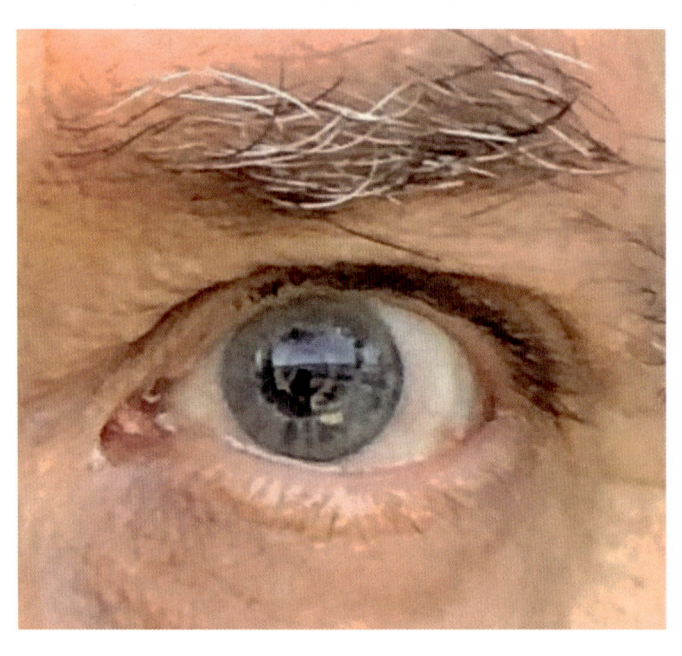

5
THE FUTURE

James Webb Space Telescope ultra-deep field, 2022

Born at the end of World War II, I have lived in a golden age. My demographic has enjoyed unearned privileges incidental to my birth—personal safety, economic opportunity, human rights, legal protections, freedom of speech and thought, quality medical care, retirement security, and more comforts not enjoyed by most people in the world today. These riches exceed even the luxuries of royalty in prior passages of human history.

But I fear my generation's gilded age is closing. It appears we are entering an inflection point in America's 250-year experiment with democracy. Those privileges feel increasingly fragile under the toxic influences of xenophobic nationalism, entrenched tribalism, white supremacy, gun rights militancy, widening wealth disparity, and resurgent anti-science theocracy.

I dearly hope that future readers will correctly regard my current worries, in 2022, as foolishly misguided, and that the American project will continue to flourish beyond today's political controversies. Let us hope that my grandchildren's age cohorts, and the generations who follow them, will find a path through today's thicket of socio-political crises. Let us hope.

I will await future's verdict as a law-abiding, tax-paying, voting American expat living snugly in Sarasota, Florida. I fear my homeland is irreversibly sliding toward an illiberalism I would not wish to be associated with. Will I be judged a gullible swallower of liberal propaganda—or a justifiably gloomy forecaster of the demise of democracy and its pleasures? I hope to live long enough to read the next chapter in American history. Thereafter, I can only hope that Seamus and Claribel may find happiness and meaning as citizens of the world they inherit. Beyond their terms, I leave to the Fates. Would that the golden age continue.

Meanwhile, I am at risk of becoming an …

AMERICAN EXPAT

midwestern farm boy
alien in my homeland
is this still my place?

Trump's America
clenched in MAGA's gun-crazed fist
I do not belong

autocracy looms
demagoguery ascends
it's all on the line

Founders' dream's deathwatch
if fake "patriots" take charge
I'll be an expat

I'm too old to flee
young ones may yet find a way
where will they call home?

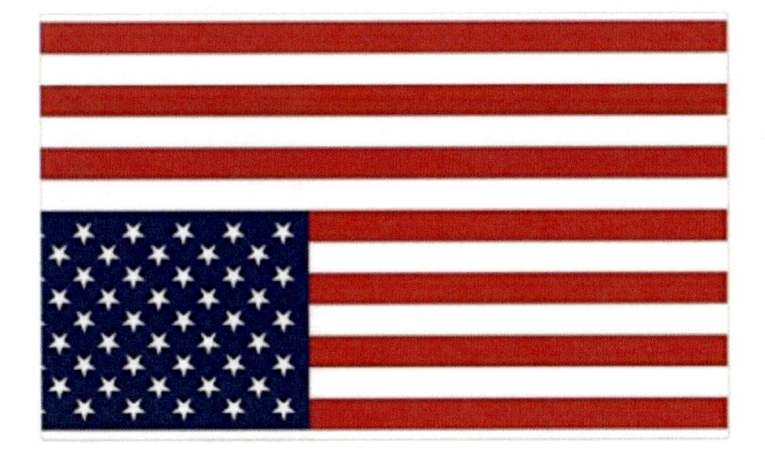

6
WRITE YOUR OWN MEMOIR

If you calculate that your life may have been mostly lived, I suspect you have considered writing your life story. Your descendants might like to know something of your lived experience, not just your birth and death dates and where to find your grave. What happened between those markers? The quest to make myself known to my descendants, born and yet unborn, inspires this memoir. I would be grateful to any of my ancestors had they done the same.

Writing one's conventional autobiography can be a daunting task.

You may find, as I did, that composing bite-size chunks is easier than tackling a book-length manuscript. The haiku quintet is only one form of snippet. Any simple, structured device can serve as the ring around your sandbox—a safe place to play. The toys in my sandbox are 85 syllables molded in the shape of a haiku quintet. Create your own toys—or play with mine.

As your snippets accumulate, assemble them into a timeline of your life, perhaps with illustrations from dusty photo albums or your iPhone's camera roll. Unless you're getting younger, today may be a good time to start.

TELL YOUR STORY

tell your life story
your forest of oak and pine
one sprout at a time

some buds may please you
others turn out to be weeds
pick and choose the best

listen to your muse
her wisdom's not of this world
she knows more than you

as your woodland grows
you are queen of your jungle
there's no higher rank

edit your new growth
keep pruning, shaping, cropping
until it feels right

Thousand-year-old bonsai tree (Crespi Bonsai Museum)

A FATHER'S DAY REGRET

what did my Dad think
about New Deal politics?
I will never know

did he fear the draft
and fighting in the next war?
I will never know

what pioneer tales
did my grandparents tell him?
I will never know

what was home-life like
in their crude prairie cabin?
I will never know

did he think about
writing his own life story?
apparently not

J. W. Dana (1874-1955), photo circa 1900

ABOUT ME

For family and friends, who are the intended and likely primary audience of this memoir, I need no introduction. For others: I am a retired mediator, psychologist, and educator living with wife Susan Moore Dana in Sarasota, Florida. Born in 1945 on a family farm in Missouri, I served, reluctantly, in the U.S. Army in Vietnam (non-combat) and Panama Canal Zone (1966-1968). Holding the PhD in psychology from University of Missouri (1977), I taught conflict management and mediation from 1978 until retirement. I founded Mediation Training Institute in 1985, acquired by Eckerd College in 2012. I have authored three books on mediation, one on secular humanism, and several volumes of haiku quintets. Five Palms Press, named for my perch overlooking Sarasota Bay, was created to share my poetic handiwork in retirement. I am the father of one and grandfather of two, to whom this memoir is dedicated. Drawing on nearly eight decades of life's experiences and misadventures, these haiku quintets may be viewed collectively as an autobiography, of sorts.

Other books—view at dandana.us/fivepalms
Available at Amazon.com and other booksellers

Post-retirement:

- *Haiku Quintets*
- *Songs of the Pandemic: World Haiku*
- *Science and Secularism: Haiku Quintets and Other Musings*
- *Common Ground: Haiku, Mediation, and Police Reform*
- *Resisting Trumpism: Haiku Quintets*
- *The Reason Revolution: Atheism, Secular Humanism, and the Collapse of Religion*

Pre-retirement

- *Managing Differences: How to Build Better Relationships at Work and Home* (MTI Publications), in seven languages
- *Conflict Resolution: Mediation Tools for Everyday Worklife* (McGraw-Hill), in multiple languages
- *Talk It Out: 4 Steps to Managing People Problems in Your Organization* (Kogan Page)

The following pages display the front covers of several English and foreign language editions of my books. Those involving conflict management and mediation were written during my career. The volumes of haiku quintets and *The Reason Revolution* were written in retirement.

HAIKU
QUINTETS
Browse
Let your mind wander
Follow it there
Repeat
DAN DANA

HAIKU
QUINTETS
Science
and
Secularism
Debunking Creationism by Science and Reason
DAN DANA

COMMON
GROUND
Haiku
Mediation
and
Police Reform
DAN DANA

HAIKU
QUINTETS
Songs
of
the
Pandemic
DAN DANA

HAIKU
QUINTETS
Resisting
Trumpism
DAN DANA

The Reason
Revolution
Atheism, Secular Humanism, and the Collapse of Religion
Dan Dana

Polish

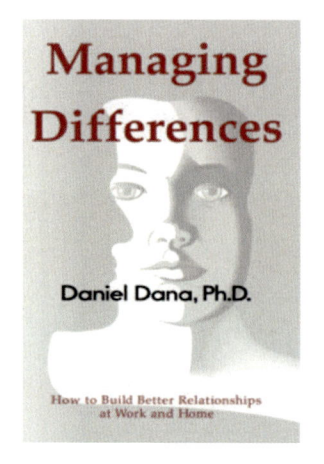

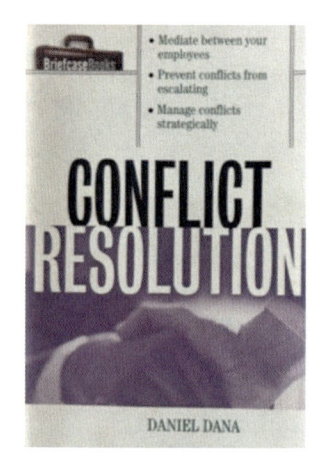

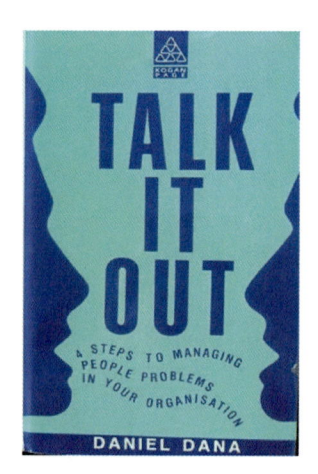

French   Spanish

Russian

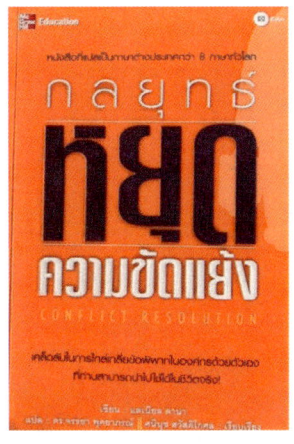

Thai

Japanese

Japanese

Korean

Dutch

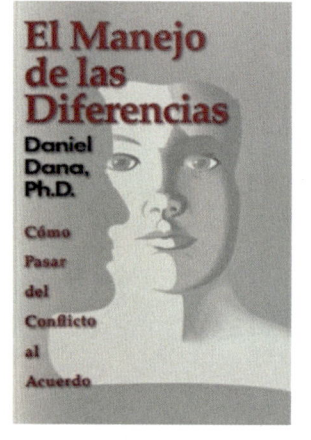

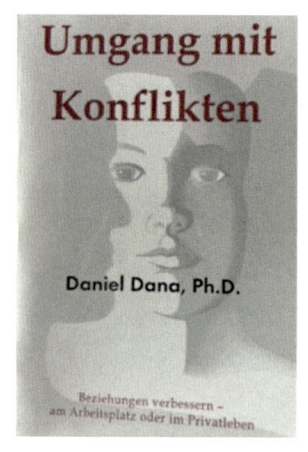

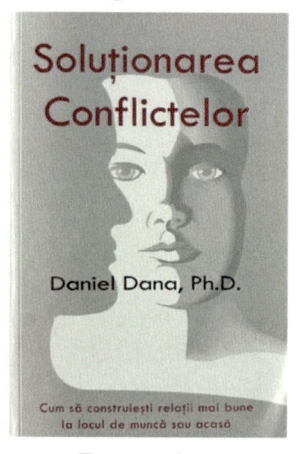

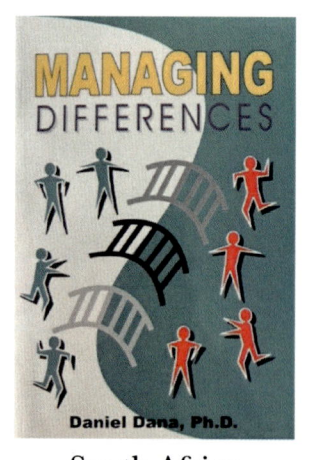

Spanish	German
Romanian	French
India	South Africa

ACKNOWLEDGEMENTS

Even one's memoir cannot be written alone.

Several friends among Lakewood Ranch Scribes and Humanists of Sarasota Bay have helped—you know who you are.

Several friends and family have shared their time and expertise—you know who you are.

And, of course, Susan—my muse in the flesh.

Special mention is due to certain friends who contributed particular expertise to this project: Mary Coleman, MD (genetics/DNA), James Burns, MD (physiology), David Tudor, PhD (statistics/probability), Dr Darrel Ray (general science), Claire Matturro (poetry), Meigs Glidewell (editing)

Cover concept: Sean Connor

Cover design: Chetan

Made in the USA
Columbia, SC
10 February 2023

56b46e78-8ad3-46a2-bbbc-99b1bd795df2R03